W9-CIG-444

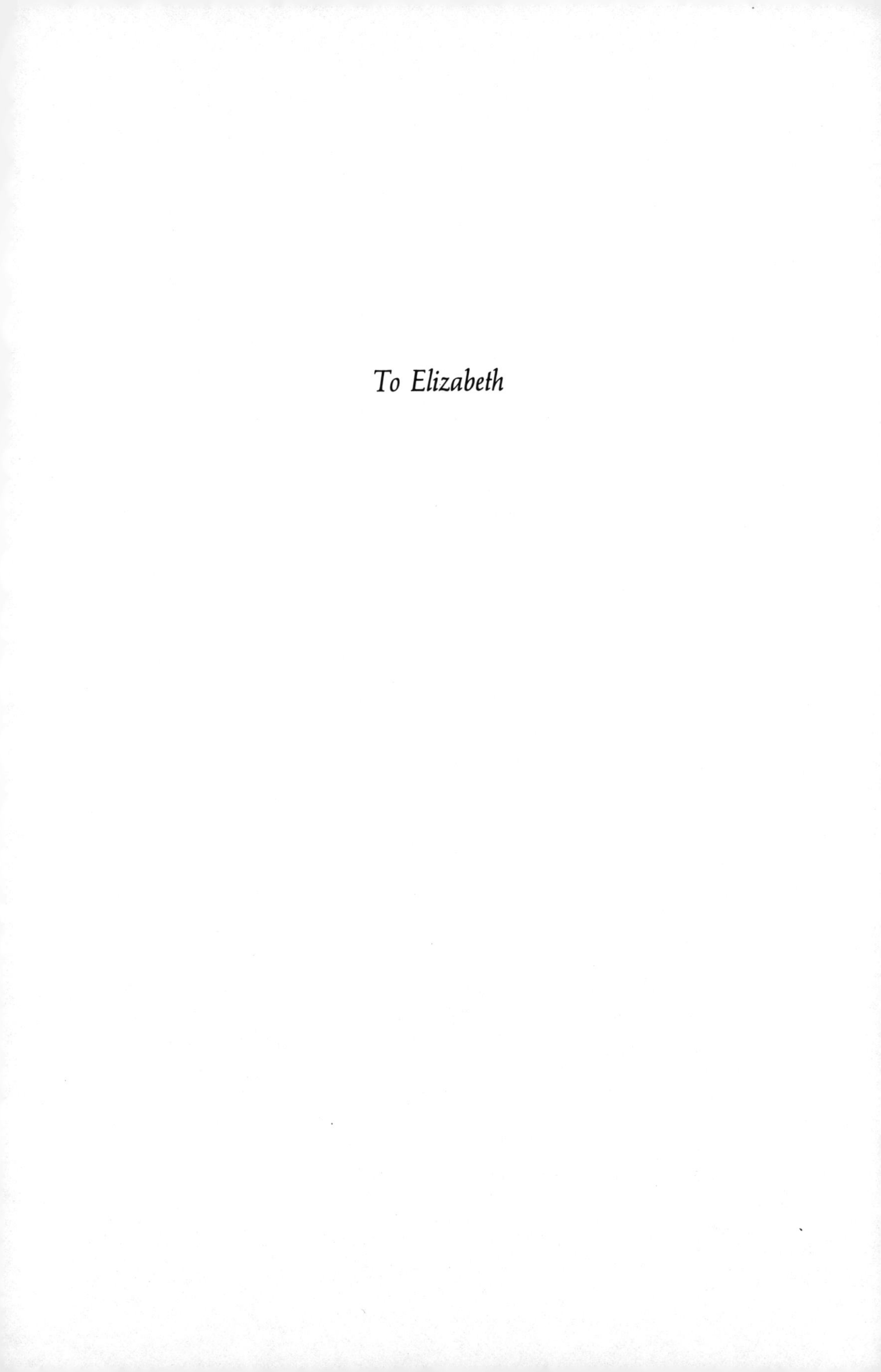

To Elizabeth

Contents

FOREWORD ix

INTRODUCTION xi

ABBREVIATIONS. xvii

BIBLIOGRAPHY 1

INDEX OF AUTHORS AND ANONYMOUS WORKS 123

INDEX OF TOPICS. 127

Foreword

The present work includes published studies on women as they appear in sixteenth and seventeenth-century Castilian literature. It is, to my knowledge, the first attempt at compiling an annotated bibliography on the subject. Among those to whom I hope it will prove useful are Hispanists devoted to study of the Golden Age, and anyone interested in teaching or writing on the subject of women in literature. It may be as helpful to see what has not been done in the field as what has. has not been done in the field as what has.

The citations include both general and particularized studies on female figures, as well as some studies in which women are mentioned only secondarily or in passing. The studies incorporated here which belong to the latter category were chosen because I felt they offered different interpretations of female figures from those already represented. In these cases, the entries deal only with those parts of the study directly pertinent to the subject of this bibliography.

In preparing this work, I made use primarily of bibliographies dated from 1946 to 1977. I did, however, include some earlier studies which seemed valuable either because they were important points of departure for future investigations, or because they offered insights not provided elsewhere. I have also included studies which appeared later than 1977 to which I had access.

Bibliographies consulted in the composition of this work include Donald W. Bleznick's *A Sourcebook for Hispanic Literature and Language: A Selected Annotated Guide to Spanish and Spanish American Bibliography, Literature, Linguistics, Journals, and Other Source Materials*, published in Philadelphia in 1974 by Temple University Press; the *Modern Language Association International Bibliography*; *Year's Work in Modern Language Studies*; periodic bibliographies in such journals as *Anales Cervantinos*, *Bulletin of the Comediantes*, *Nueva Revista de Filología Hispánica*, *Revista de Filología Española*, *Revista de Literatura*, and *Studies in Philology*; and specialized bibliographies on particular authors, genres, and topics. Anyone interested in theses and dissertations on the subject should consult David J. Billick's "Women in Hispanic Literature: A Checklist of Doctoral Dissertations and Master's Theses, 1905-1975," in *Women*

Foreword

Studies Abstracts, 6 (Summer 1977), 1-11, as well as the same author's "Theses and Dissertations on Women in Hispanic Literature: A Supplement for 1976-77," in WSA, 7 (Summer-Fall 1978), 1-3.

This type of study is, of course, by its very nature always incomplete, and I make no claim to having covered exhaustively the area delimited above. I would be grateful for additional information from any who are aware of other pertinent studies so that I might update the present bibliography. It is my hope that this undertaking will encourage other interested persons to supplement it with related studies, such as a bibliography on women writers in Golden Age Spain.

I wish to express my gratitude to the women in the Interlibrary Loan Department of the University of Wyoming for their more than generous and persistent efforts on my behalf.

M. Louise Salstad
University of Wyoming

Introduction

The medieval Mary-Eve antithesis continues in Spanish literature of the sixteenth and seventeenth centuries, both in conceptualized statements about women, and in individual feminine figures; figures like Cervantes's Zoraida or Tirso's María de Molina on the one hand, Lope's Casandra of El castigo sin venganza or any of numerous pícaras on the other. Besides the contrasting Biblical prototypes, Golden Age writers like to use as analogues famous types from classical literature, such as Lucretia, Portia, and Penelope on the positive side, Circe and the sirens on the negative.

The debate between the detractors and defenders of women acquires a broader base, however, in the sixteenth century, due in great part to Erasmus and his followers. To the medieval preoccupation with woman's moral qualities is added the issue of her intellectual capacity. Woman is still considered inferior to man in this respect. It is unanimously agreed by her male expositors that nature has equipped her exclusively for the domestic sphere. Those writers who are, relatively speaking, the most liberal or humane in their views believe that women who show a capacity for and interest in learning should not be denied the opportunity for the same, but it should be imparted within the confines of the home, and rather than an end in itself, it should be a means to greater piety and benefit to the family. The humanists recognize the importance of the role of woman in the improvement of society, but her influence is to make itself felt indirectly. Another idea which emerges in the sixteenth century is that a woman is basically responsible for maintaining her own virtue.

All of these issues: woman's moral character, moral freedom, and education, continue to be explored in the seventeenth century. On the last point there does not seem to be much progress. With regard to moral freedom, however, the view that a woman, to be virtuous, must be able to choose proper conduct for herself rather than have it forced upon her, finds several exponents, the most notable, perhaps, Miguel de Cervantes. Another freedom, which gains widespread support among seventeenth-century writers, is the right of a woman to choose her own marriage partner. This is also the century in which a woman herself, apparently for the first time in Spain, writes in defense of her sex. María de Zayas y Sotomayor claims inherent spiritual and intellectual equality for men and women, accusing men of purposely keeping women weak and ignorant.

The feminist issue per se becomes a topic of lively interest. The idea that love and marriage are woman's essential and proper role and the surest means to her fulfillment comes under question. María de Zayas rejects the notion; the dramatists, after presenting many cases of women who resist it, reaffirm it in the end by showing that these women were contravening the God-given order of nature, as well as that of society. In virtually every case, the women involved are eventually reconciled to marriage and the subordination of all other aspirations to the overriding power of love for a man. Nevertheless, the comediantes do deal sympathetically with some of the problems and frustrations faced by women in a male-dominated society.

The defense of women, it has been said by such critics as María Rosa Lida de Malkiel, becomes a subgenre in the Golden Age. Interestingly enough, certain classical figures which serve as important references in this defense, such as Lucretia and Dido, are themselves swept into the controversy surrounding women, rallying their own vehement champions and detractors.

There is a great disparity of views among literary historians and critics as to the precise attitude toward women of many Golden Age writers, notable examples being Fray Luis de León, Santa Teresa de Jesús, Miguel de Cervantes, and Tirso de Molina. Luis de León's La perfecta casada (1583), a relatively brief but very influential work, which was in its turn influenced by Juan Luis Vives's De Institutione Feminae Christianae (1523), is criticized for its negative concept of women's intellectual and moral capacity, for keeping women down, yet praised as representing a forward step in the evaluation of women. It merits such praise, among other reasons, because it is the first serious work by a respected theologian dedicated to the subject of woman, specifically, the married woman.

Santa Teresa, it is said, concurs, and rightly so, with the view of women as naturally weak creatures (not only in the physical but even, and especially, in the moral sense), who need all the help they can get to escape falling prey to the various delusions of the devil. It is also noted, however, that she affirms women's frequent surpassing of men in the spiritual life and predicts that there will be many surprises on the day of judgment for those who hold women to be inferior to men.

Cervantes is interpreted by some as a misogynist or at best, as a conventional thinker who sees women as weak and in need of men's help in order to remain virtuous. Others see him as a writer who was ahead of his time in upholding woman's rights and affirming her personality.

Tirso de Molina is, depending upon the critic, profoundly pessimistic regarding women's moral capacity, inevitably so since he was a friar; sympathetic to women without idealizing them; or a precursor of the women's liberation movement. Not even in the case of Francisco de Quevedo, who is usually viewed as a virulent misogynist, are all the critics in agreement.

Such disparity of views is due in part, I believe, to certain failures of the critics. Among these are the failure to consider the demands of the genre or the writer's need to gratify or placate a particular audience. Another is the failure to distinguish between opinions, often clichés, voiced by a certain character or by the narrator and the attitude conveyed by the work as a whole, in which the presentation of particular female figures is probably more revelatory of the writer's deeply held personal views. The inevitable biases of the critic are also partly accountable for the disparity, and a final important factor is the complexity of certain writers and their own human ambivalence regarding women.

The underlying aim or philosophy of a genre determines to a great extent the way in which woman is presented. At one extreme we find the essentially negative characterizations of the picaresque and celestinesque novels and satirical or _costumbrista_ works; at the other, the idealizations of many pastoral novels, the chivalry novels, and certain kinds of _novela_. In the picaresque novels with a male protagonist, women are both a means or instrument for men's material advantage and the gratification of their sexual appetite, as well as a temptation and a snare for men, the cause of their perdition. Literary historians disagree as to the first picaresque novel with a female protagonist, some claiming this honor for Francisco Delicado's _La lozana andaluza_ (1528); others, for Francisco López de Ubeda's _La pícara Justina_ (1605), and even in the latter case there are those who deny that the heroine is a true _pícara_. In works such as these, women are essentially similar to their male counterparts, motivated by the need to survive, self-interest, and, at times, pleasure in hoodwinking others, though the _pícara_'s cleverness assumes special forms because of her sex.

Fernando de Rojas's _Tragicomedia de Calisto y Melibea_, more popularly known as _La Celestina_ (1499), produced numerous progeny; hypocritical, greedy, and lecherous go-betweens, none of whom, however, attains the stature of her prototype.

Quevedo's satirical diatribes give the impression that he considers all members of the feminine sex, and especially old women, as ridiculous or repugnant and always fraudulent.

In the pastoral novel, woman, in accord with its Neoplatonic philosophy, is the most perfect earthly image of eternal beauty and thus, the object of cult and veneration. In the chivalry books, the doctrine of courtly love makes her the object of the knight's total devotion--even adoration, the inspirer of his noble deeds. The _novelas_ of Zayas, which may be considered as belonging to the subgenre of defense of women, present female protagonists who are usually innocent martyrs of male cruelty and oppression.

Some of Cervantes's more romantic _novelas_ exalt women who maintain their innocence in the midst of the world's temptations or tribulations, or who serve as a kind of mentor to a man or as the instrument of his salvation. Calderón's theological and metaphysical plays frequently present women in this last role, on a more symbolic level than Cervantes.

Nevertheless, the feminine sex in these last writers, as in many others, cannot be limited to a certain type or to a single cluster of defining traits. As the Golden Age progresses it might be said that, side by side with the prolongation of the traditional antitheses, there is an ever greater variety and complexity in the presentation of women. This tendency is notable particularly in the great _comediantes_ and in certain works of Cervantes. Lope de Vega, the Golden Age dramatist who, it has been said by such literary critics as Agustín de Amezúa y Mayo, Ricardo del Arco, and Elena Laborde, possesses the most direct and vital knowledge of women, gives us in incipient form some very perceptive psychological characterizations. It is Cervantes, however, who depicts in Dorotea of _Don Quixote_ the female figure who is perhaps the most complete woman in all of Spanish Golden Age literature.

Among the qualities for which women in general seem to be most highly valued are purity, beauty--based on the Petrarchan construct, prudence (the implied contradiction in the title of Tirso's _La prudencia en la mujer_ indicates that while it was valued, it was not expected), and the demonstration of unstinting and self-sacrificing love. Women who are not interested in love must be converted; those who prove incapable of selfless love are usually punished. Conversely, if there is any justification or pardon for a woman's errors in the view of these writers, it is love. Indeed, the woman in love is the single most ubiquitous type in the literature. Obedience and patience are also valued on a theoretical level, but these virtues are usually manifested in secondary female figures. In practice, Spanish Golden Age writers admire spunk, the initiative and spirit displayed by a woman who knows what she wants and goes after it, provided her goal be worthy. Usually this means marriage to the man of her choice or the defense of her honor.

Qualities for which women are most often denounced are ambition for power, hypocrisy (ironically enough, given their subordinate position), lasciviousness, greed, pedantry or "excessive" zeal for learning, and the desire to be independent of men. Astuteness or slyness is viewed as a typically feminine trait. It differs from discretion or prudence, among other ways, in that it is characteristic of the underdog, be she the _dama_ of a _comedia_ or _novela_ or a _pícara_, and it is viewed with delighted amazement, vituperation, or alarm according to the context.

Of course one must be wary of drawing hasty conclusions about the real situation of women in Golden Age Spain based on the literature alone, since it has its own aims, conventions, and tabus, and since its feminine figures are often influenced at least as much by literary tradition as by real life. The disagreement among critics over the relative importance of these two sources of influence for the mujer vestida de hombre provides a salutary warning. The relative lack of certain types, such as the mother, the middle-class woman, and the laboring woman, obviously does not reflect the actual state of affairs. Not all the feminine inhabitants of Spain's cities were either aristocratic ladies or prostitutes and swindlers; the majority of country women did not live in such idyllic circumstances as many of Lope's comedias would make it seem. Nor were husbands regularly killing their wives on the suspicion that they had become unfaithful or in some way besmirched their honor. Sometimes certain atypical works of literature themselves help to balance what would otherwise be a very distorted picture. A case in point are the novelas of Mariana de Carvajal, which leave a quite different impression of the relationships between father and daughter or brother and sister from that conveyed by Zayas, for example, or by much of Golden Age theater.

Still, with a little soft-focussing one can reasonably conclude certain things about Spanish women and their way of life in the sixteenth and seventeenth centuries. One can deduce, for instance, that their level of education was meager on the whole; that their life style and life options were quite severely limited and that this situation gave rise to psychological and social problems. One can also derive from the literature some fairly accurate information about the customs, routines, and fashions of women, particularly of the upper classes; and one can perceive some of the deep-seated values of the society with respect to women, even if the situations mirroring those values are exaggerated.

Abbreviations

The following list includes abbreviations of certain periodicals and collections of essays cited more than once in the bibliography.

ACer Anales Cervantinos

Actas Actas del Tercer Congreso Internacional de Hispanistas. Edited by Carlos H. Magis. México: El Colegio de México, 1970.

Archivum Archivum (Oviedo, Spain)

ArH Archivo Hispalense: Revista Histórica, Literaria y Artística (Seville)

BACL Boletín de la Academia Cubana de la Lengua

BBMP Boletín de la Biblioteca Menéndez y Pelayo

BCom Bulletin of the Comediantes

BH Bulletin Hispanique

BHS Bulletin of Hispanic Studies [Formerly Bulletin of Spanish Studies]

BRAE Boletín de la Real Academia Española

CA Cuadernos Americanos

CHA Cuadernos Hispanoamericanos: Revista Mensual de Cultura Hispánica (Madrid)

Critical Essays Critical Essays on the Theatre of Calderón. Edited by Bruce W. Wardropper. New York: New York University Press, 1965.

DdY Diario de Yucatán (Mérida, México)

Abbreviations

DMar Diario de la Marina (Havana, Cuba)

ENac El Nacional (México)

EstLit La Estafeta Literaria: Revista Quincenal de Libros, Artes y Espectáculos

Estudios Estudios (Madrid)

Estudios hispánicos Estudios hispánicos: Homenaje a Archer M. Huntington. Wellesley, Mass.: Wellesley College, 1952.

Estudios literarios Estudios literarios de hispanistas norteamericanos dedicados a Helmut Hatzfeld con motivo de su 80 aniversario. Edited by J. M. Sola-Solé, et al. Barcelona: Hispam, 1974.

ExTL Explicación de Textos Literarios

Filología Filología (Buenos Aires)

HAG Homenaje al Excmo. Sr. Dr. D. Emilio Alarcos García. Vol. 2. Valladolid: Sever-Cuesta, 1965.

Hispania Hispania (U. of Mass.)

Hispano Hispanófila

HR Hispanic Review

HRM Homenaje a Rodríguez-Moñino. 2 vols. Madrid: Castalia, 1966.

Ibero Iberoromania: Zeitschrift für Sprachen und Literaturen von Spanien, Portugal und Iberoamerika

KRQ Kentucky Romance Quarterly

La Celestina y su contorno La Celestina y su contorno social: Actas del I Congreso Internacional sobre La Celestina. Edited by Manuel Criado de Val. Barcelona: Borrás, 1977.

MLN Modern Language Notes

MLR Modern Language Review

Neophil Neophilologus

Nov Novedades (México)

NRFH Nueva Revista de Filología Hispánica

PMLA Publications of the Modern Language Association of America

Abbreviations

PPNCFL *Proceedings of the Pacific Northwest Council on Foreign Languages*

PSA *Papeles de Son Armadans*

RCEH *Revista Canadiense de Estudios Hispánicos*

RdA *Revista de América*

REH *Revista de Estudios Hispánicos*

RF *Romanische Forschungen*

RHM *Revista Hispánica Moderna: Columbia University Hispanic Studies*

RJ *Romanistisches Jahrbuch*

RL *Revista de Literatura*

RLC *Revue de Littérature Comparée*

RomN *Romance Notes*

RR *Romanic Review*

SLGZ *Spanische Literatur im Goldenen Zeitalter: Fritz Schalk zum 70 Geburtstag*. Edited by Horst Baader and E. Loos. Frankfurt, West Germany: Vittorio Klostermann, 1973.

SPh *Studies in Philology*

Stylo *Stylo* (Temuco, Chile)

Thesaurus *Thesaurus: Boletín del Instituto Caro y Cuervo*

Wort und Text *Wort und Text: Festschrift für Fritz Schalk*. Edited by Harri Meier and H. Sckommodau. Frankfurt, West Germany: Vittorio Klostermann, 1963.

Bibliography

1 Agheana, Ion T. "Guillén de Castro's Jimena: An Exemplary Character and Its Flaw." BCom, 29 (Spring 1977), 34-38.
The character of Guillén de Castro's Jimena is fundamentally different from the Jimena of the ballads. What she projects most forcefully throughout the drama is her social self. Her strong sense of justice and duty makes her exemplary, but her indiscriminate adherence to social laws, even when they are inhuman, makes her pitiable.

2 Allen, John J. "Lope de Vega y la imagenería petrarquista de belleza femenina." Estudios literarios, pp. 5-23.
Imagery of feminine beauty in Spanish Golden Age poetry is based primarily on Petrarch. Allen traces Lope's trajectory in this respect, beginning with the first edition of Rimas and ending with La Circe.

3 Allué y Morer, Fernando. "Galiana de Toledo." Clavileño, 7, no. 37 (1956), 27-34.
The author presents fragments from various works of Golden Age literature in which the legendary Moorish princess, Galiana, is extraordinarily beautiful.

4 _____. "Mujeres en Lope." Poesía Española, no. 187 (July 1968), pp. 8-15.
Lope's Laurel de Apolo includes references to twelve women poets who wrote in Castilian: Ana de Ayala, Clara de Barrionuevo, Ana de Castro Egas, Feliciana Enríquez de Guzmán, Cristobalina Fernández de Alarcón, Bernarda Ferreira de la Cerda, Juliana Morella, Isabel de Rivadeneira, Jerónima de Velasco, María de Zayas y Sotomayor, Ana de Zuazo, and Laurencia de Zurita. All but Juliana Morella are hidalgas, and all are praised by Lope for their verses, beauty, discretion, or intellectual capacity. Lope is the only source in some cases for what biographical and bibliographical information we possess on these women writers.

*5 Alonso, María Rosa. "El tema de la mujer hasta Quevedo." Cuadernos de la Facultad de Filosofía y Letras, Madrid, 1 (1935), pp. 17-26.

Bibliography

6 Alvarez, Guzmán. *El amor en la novela picaresca española*. The Hague: Van Goor, 1958.

Novels with female protagonists discussed by Alvarez are López de Ubeda's *La pícara Justina*, Salas Barbadillo's *La hija de Celestina*, and Castillo Solórzano's *La garduña de Sevilla*. The author compares and contrasts the personalities, behavior, and relationships with men of the respective heroines, Justina, Elena, and Rufina.

7 _____. *Le thème de la femme dans la picaresque espagnole*. Groningen, Netherlands: J. B. Wolters, 1955.

After pointing out the great contrast between the portrayal of women in the picaresque novel and in other literary genres, especially in regard to chastity, the author comments on female characters in *Lazarillo*, Alemán's *Guzmán de Alfarache*, and Quevedo's *Buscón*. He concludes that women and love are in the background in this genre, and that woman is basically sought by the *pícaro* to satisfy his appetite. The heroine of the best known novel with a female protagonist, López de Ubeda's *La pícara Justina*, is not so much a *pícara* as a prankster and avenging angel.

8 Amezúa y Mayo, Agustín G. de. *Cervantes, creador de la novela corta española*. 2 vols. Madrid: Consejo Superior de Investigaciones Científicas, 1956-58. See especially 1, pp. 237-43.

The ideas regarding women found scattered throughout Cervantes's works align him with the misogynistic writers. With respect to the *Novelas ejemplares*, the feminine figures are in general beautiful, attractive, and *simpáticas*, but, with the exception of Preciosa of *La gitanilla*, Leonisa of *El amante liberal* (one of the best drawn characters of the collection), and Constanza of *La ilustre fregona*, they are unoriginal, vague, and lacking in a strong personality. Cervantes is more successful in the portrayal of women of mature age, such as doña Rodríguez of *Don Quixote* and Marialonso of *El celoso extremeño*.

9 _____. "Doña María de Zayas: Notas críticas." *Opúsculos histórico-literarios*. Vol. 2. Madrid: Consejo Superior de Investigaciones Científicas, 1951, pp. 1-47.

Zayas continues the Spanish novelistic and dramatic tradition of portraying women as ingenious, passionate, valiant, and intrepid, qualities which she presents as inspired by the force of love. Such depiction truthfully reflects the character of real Spanish women of the period, though Zayas's use of the male disguise is often lacking in verisimilitude.

A dominant sentiment in Zayas's works is a deeply rooted

and intransigent feminism; nearly all her novelas serve to vindicate the women of her time. Although her defense of women is not blind or absolute, she represents men as basically responsible for women's ignorance and weakness, whereas their native intelligence and other natural gifts are essentially no different from those of men. Her comedia, La traición en la amistad, contradicts this defensive feminine impulse.

10 _____. Lope de Vega en sus cartas: Introducción al epistolario de Lope de Vega Carpio. Vol. 2. Madrid: Escelicer, 1940, pp. 547-66, 664-67.

Lope's frank and progressive feminism in his dramatic, lyric, and novelistic works is remarkable in comparison to the misogynistic attitude of most of his peers. He deals with all the controversies of the time regarding women, such as their superiority or inferiority vis-à-vis men, and feminine education. Lope treats the first question with prudent eclecticism. He resolves the second in an apparently restrictive manner but still shows enthusiasm for the woman who cultivates her understanding. Lope's favorite type is the woman in love, a state which he sees as natural and proper to woman. The fusion of admiration for woman and recognition of her weak and imperfect nature engenders in Lope a new type of feminism, one born from an indulgent comprehension of woman's soul, which is rarely constant and logical. The true substance of Lope's feminism is to be sought not in his theater but in his love poems, where woman is the all-embracing cosmos.

Nevertheless, Lope's letters reveal a different attitude. While not so inflexibly or harshly misogynistic as some writers of the time, he expresses resentment, suspicion, and fear of women.

*11 Anaya Solórzano, Soledad. "Mujeres en la obra de Cervantes." Homenaje de la Universidad Femenina en el IV Centenario de Cervantes. México: Universidad Femenina de México, 1947, unpaginated.

12 Apráiz, Angel de. Doña Inés de Castro en el teatro castellano. Vitoria, Spain: Domingo Sar, 1911.

Spanish dramatists, not content with earlier endings in which Inés's assassins are punished and she is declared by Pedro to be his legitimate wife, pay the highest tribute to her misfortunes by having her corpse crowned and her hands kissed by the conspirators. Among the works in Castilian dealt with by Apráiz are the tragedies of Fray Jerónimo Bermúdez, Nise lastimosa and Nise laureada, of which the former portrays Inés as a loving mother and a woman overcome by terror with the precognition of her impending death; two *romances* included in the *Primera parte del romancero y tragedias de Gabriel Lobo Lasso de la Vega*; the poem "La Infanta coronada" by Juan Suárez de Alarcón; the *Tragedia famosa de doña Inés de Castro, Reina de Portugal* by Mexía de la Cerda, which again portrays the heroine as continually accompanied by fear and inquietude; and *Reinar después de morir* by Luis Vélez de Guevara, which depicts Inés as a sorrowfully moving figure who, while jealous and fearful of her rival, is strong and courageous when she has to defend her love of spouse and children.

13 Aragonés, Juan Emilio. "La figura de Santa Teresa en el teatro español." *EstLit*, nos. 453-54 (15 October 1970), pp. 54-55.

Lope de Vega, the first to dramatize the figure of Teresa, wrote three plays about her, of which two, *La Madre Teresa de Jesús* and *Vida y muerte de Santa Teresa de Jesús*, are extant. Two other Golden Age plays about Teresa are Luis Vélez de Guevara's *La bienaventurada Madre Santa Teresa de Jesús, monja descalza de Nuestra Señora del Carmen*, and Juan Bautista Diamante's *Santa Teresa de Jesús*.

14 Araujo Costa, Luis. "Margarita del centenario: La pastora Marcela." *DdY* (8 June 1947), p. 8.

The most sublime part of the *Quixote* is the Platonic discourse Cervantes puts in the mouth of the shepherdess Marcela, as discreet as she is beautiful. Her speech leaves fixed forever the character of Spain and her women.

15 Arce de Vázquez, Margot. *Garcilaso de la Vega: Contribución al estudio de la lírica española del siglo XVI*. Second Edition. Río Piedras: Ediciones de la Universidad de Puerto Rico, 1961. See especially pp. 25, 83-85.

The high-spirited and energetic shepherdess Camila of "Egloga II," who defends her rights as a woman, could be a predecessor of Cervantes's Marcela.

Isabel Freyre fills Garcilaso's poetry with her beauty and disdain, but there is not a single allusion to her moral qualities. Garcilaso always shows respect and *simpatía* for women. One of the qualities he most esteems in them is wisdom or *ingenio*. His feminine ideal is perhaps summarized in verses 1417-18 of "Egloga II," which describe the bride of the Duke of Alba as sweet, pure, beautiful, wise, and *honesta*.

16 Arco, Ricardo del. "La 'dueña' en la literatura española." *RL*, 3, no. 6 (1953), 293-343.

The *dueña* becomes an obsession of numerous Golden Age

writers, who represent her as an object of jest and ridicule or as a perverse social manifestation. Arco discusses the type in writers such as Cervantes, Quiñones de Benavente, Quevedo, and Calderón. Cervantes, who gives us an immortal model in doña Rodríguez of Don Quixote, employs a subtle irony in his portrayal of the type, without descending to the vulgar comparisons found in other writers. Quevedo, who refers to the dueña copiously and with the greatest variety of epithets and similes, turns his depictions into caricatures. At the end of the seventeenth century the dueña loses her social significance and her notable position in literature.

17 _____. "Más sobre Tirso de Molina y el medio social." BRAE, 33 (January-April 1953), 19-72; 33 (May-August 1953), 243-93. See especially pp. 56 ff., 271 ff.

Arco cites passages from Tirso which he considers indicative of the dramatist's attitude toward women and their lot. He concludes that Tirso is sympathetic to women without idealizing them.

18 _____. "Mujer, amor, celos y matrimonio vistos por Cervantes." BBMP, 28 (1952), 133-65.

The author selects ideas from his book La sociedad española en las obras de Cervantes.

19 _____. La sociedad española en las obras de Cervantes. Madrid: Patronato del IV Centenario del Nacimiento de Cervantes, 1951. See especially Ch. IX, pp. 237-54, and Chs. XIII, XIV, XVIII, and XXII passim.

Arco examines Cervantes's portrayal of women in his novelistic and dramatic works. In comparison to other writers, Cervantes is indulgent with women. He produced one of the most varied female portrait galleries in Spanish art and created types which, though not traced so firmly as Lope's and Tirso's, are nevertheless very human and verisimilar. Because of his exemplarism, the unchaste woman is virtually nonexistent in Cervantes. Nearly all his female protagonists are incarnations of true love, and in all his female creations, feeling predominates. The nobler women, however, are endowed with such traits as intelligence, discreción, strength, and valor as well.

20 _____. La sociedad española en las obras dramáticas de Lope de Vega. Madrid: Escelicer, 1942. See especially Ch. X.

Whereas Calderón's female characters are abstract entities, Lope's are warmly human. He presents the loving devotion of women more beautifully and intimately than any other dramatist except Shakespeare, making them, and not men, the heroic souls. While Tirso is usually a detractor of women, and Alarcón makes them subsidiary to men (his real focus of interest) Lope is always the friend of women. He praises them highly, and even his censure and satire involve a substratum of adhesion which he cannot conceal.

With regard to specific types and issues, Lope establishes definitively the type of the doncella who dresses as a man in order to reconquer a lost love or defend her honor; favors a moderate amount of ingenio in women but opposes the bluestocking; supports women's desire for more freedom in love; and offers no example of the exalted mother figure. The mother was usually deliberately omitted from Golden Age comedy because, if given a dignified role, she would hamstring the plot development; and if she were made to accommodate the action, her sacred name and position would be degraded.

21 Arjona, J. Homero. "El disfraz varonil en Lope de Vega." BH, 39 (1937), 120-45.

In 113 of 460 comedias examined, Lope uses the male disguise more than any other dramatist, including Tirso. Calderón and Alarcón use it less often than most. Arjona identifies and discusses six kinds of situations in which Lope uses the device, the most common being a young woman's abandoning home to follow a lover or spouse. He also treats Lope's technique in handling the device, the use he makes of it in the plays, its censure by moralists, and its relation to historical reality.

22 Armas, Frederick A. de. The Invisible Mistress: Aspects of Feminism and Fantasy in the Golden Age. Charlottesville, Va.: Biblioteca Siglo de Oro, 1976.

Armas discusses at length various comedias and novelas which utilize the Invisible Mistress plot, including Lope's La viuda valenciana; Tirso's Amar por señas, Quien calla, otorga, and La celosa de sí misma; Calderón's La dama duende; Alonso de Castillo Solórzano's "Los efectos que hace amor" from Los alivios de Casandra; and Ana Caro's El conde Partinuplés. Common to all is the presentation of a fantasy or burla created by a woman in order to liberate herself from her physical captivity and mental torment, and to instill in the man the old Christian chivalric ideals. The accepted social roles are reversed, the woman being the active element, the man, a passive figure who comes to accept and love her creation. Woman's fantasy is her only means of self-expression, a way to demonstrate her humanity to man. This is not feminism in the modern sense; woman does not wish to be free and equal to man but simply to perform what she sees as her proper role. She wants to be, not an object of suspicion, but one of admiration, a motivation for heroism. It is in the acceptance or rejection of a woman's actions derived from her fantasy that Golden Age writers define their attitude toward feminism.

23 Ashcom, B. B. "Concerning 'la mujer en hábito de hombre' in the comedia." HR, 28 (January 1960), 43-62.

The article is a critical review of Carmen Bravo-Villasante's La mujer vestida de hombre en el teatro español (see entry 44). Besides classical antiquity and Italian novelle, epico-romances, and drama, Ashcom finds another possible model for the type, French medieval chansons de geste and romans. Bravo-Villasante neglects Luis Vélez de Guevara, whom Ashcom considers the greatest exponent of la mujer varonil in various forms. Ashcom believes the theme cannot be considered merely a literary creation, since there were many known cases of transvestism. He considers the mujer varonil abnormal in whatever context and finds the Lesbian motif implicit in most plots involving the type.

24 Atlee, A. F. Michael. "Concepto y ser metafórico de Dulcinea." ACer, 15 (1976), 223-36.

The most popular of the numerous interpretations of Dulcinea and her role in the Quixote is that she and Don Quixote's love for her serve to parody courtly love. For Casalduero (see entry 57), Dulcinea is pure idea; for Madariaga, glory; for Emilio Goggio, prime mover of all Don Quixote's actions. These opinions initiated the investigations resulting in Atlee's thesis, that Dulcinea is a metaphor for the Aristotelian concept of God which arose during the Middle Ages in the form of courtly love.

25 Avalle-Arce, Juan Bautista. La novela pastoril española. Second Edition. Madrid: Ediciones Istmo, 1974.

With respect to Montemayor's La Diana, the critic observes that the wise Felicia's lineage is related to that of Urganda of Amadís.

Cervantes's La Galatea displays ambivalence in the theme of woman. According to the Platonic pastoral tradition, feminine beauty is the earthly reflection of divine perfection, but in Cervantes's novel, this evaluation is open to personal opinion and individual circumstance. The Marcela-Grisóstomo episode in the Quixote recalls that of Gelasia and Galercio in the Galatea, but what in Gelasia's sonnet is a barely sketched argumentation becomes, in the Quixote, an eloquent and complete defense of woman's free will in issues of love, a speech which is given vital validity through the integral will revealed by Marcela. Also related is the Leandra episode, but where Marcela and Gelasia use their free will to continue being something (free women who are not in love), Leandra uses hers to stop being something (a modest village girl).

26 Azorín. "El caso Marcela." DdY (18 June 1947), pp. 3, 6.
Among the ten or twelve women who form the spiritual atmosphere of the Quixote and with whom the men cannot compete, Marcela--enigma, psychological problem, symbol--stands out. The solitude which she desires, however, is not so austere as she seems to think. Were she confronted with the immense, unpeopled space of the New World, she would, for all her independence, retreat before it.

27 _____. "Cervantes y Zoraida." DdY (17 July 1947), pp. 3, 9.
In her solitude and idleness Zoraida strikes one as a curious and restless woman. Cervantes wishes to portray her as candid and ingenuous, but he in fact presents her as artful and a consummate actress. Once the absolute mistress of the household, she supposedly accustoms herself without difficulty to a life of poverty and uncertainty. Camila of "El curioso impertinente," on the other hand, falls, a victim to the absolute. Yet she wins our affection, while Zoraida does not.

28 _____. "Dulcinea, peligrosa." DdY (9 August 1947), pp. 3, 8.
Woman dominates man in the Quixote, the female types being more vigorous than the male. Given this pattern, as well as woman's preponderance in Spanish life, Dulcinea was a danger for Cervantes. If he insisted too much on her portrait, she rather than Don Quixote would become the protagonist of the novel. Cervantes avoided this by making her simply a name instead of a figure of flesh and blood. For even greater surety he created two crude figures, that of the labradora of Toboso and that of the village lass encountered on the road, who intervene whenever the reader wants to concretize the concept of Dulcinea.

29 _____. "Leandra y Augusta." DdY (10 May 1947), p. 3.
Cervantes's Leandra and Galdós's Augusta are alike in their beauty, intelligence, and wealth. Both have a tendency to fall in love with what is unusual or extraordinary, and both believe in their heart of hearts in the value of the unpremeditated experience, because to such they owe the few joys of their existence. Augusta, however, a woman of the nineteenth century, is able to intellectually articulate this conviction, whereas Leandra could never do so.

30 Bagby, Albert I., Jr. "*La loçana andaluza* vista en su perspectiva donjuanesca." *Hispano*, no. 35 (January 1969), pp. 19-25.

Francisco Delicado's Lozana is too complex a character to be stereotyped. Besides possessing traits common to the Celestina type, the courtesan, and the *pícara*, she is very much of a feminine don Juan in several respects. These include her desire for sexual pleasure, her manipulation of others, her role as initiator in relations with the opposite Juan, she remains proud and arrogant to the very end.

31 _____. "La primera novela picaresca española." *La Torre*, 68 (1970), 83-100.

Delicado's *La lozana andaluza* is the first picaresque novel, and its protagonist, labeled by critics a simple prostitute, Celestina, courtesan, *rufiana*, procuress, or thief, is really a complete *pícara* in the best tradition of the type. In spite of the ups and downs of her existence and the gradual improvement in her situation, she is morally and spiritually always the same. Her chief attribute is ingenuity, one of the most important qualities of the *pícaro*. Her practice of using sexual stratagems on men, not out of erotic desire but in order to survive, is typical of the *pícara*, as is her philosophy of life: to take advantage of people's stupidity in order to live as well as possible.

32 Bandera, Cesáreo. *Mimesis conflictiva: Ficción literaria y violencia en Cervantes y Calderón*. Madrid: Gredos, 1975. See pp. 184-99.

Bandera discusses Rosaura's relation to Basilio and her connection to the central relationship of Calderón's *La vida es sueño*, that between Basilio and Segismundo. Rosaura, who is with respect to Segismundo what he is with respect to Basilio, has an ambivalent role, for besides introducing confusion and violence into the palace, she is the only way to peace.

33 Barbero, Teresa. "María de Zayas y Sotomayor o la picaresca cortesana." *EstLit*, no. 527 (1 November 1973), pp. 24-25.

In her incredibly advanced social and intellectual defense of woman, Zayas breaks with all conventions and prejudices sanctioned by an almost medieval society. She portrays starkly the only weapons--and those not the most *honestas*--which women have been allowed to use in defense of their liberty as human beings in the face of male oppression.

34 Barrenechea, Ana María. "*La ilustre fregona* como ejemplo de estructura novelesca cervantina." *Filología*, 7 (1961), 13-32.

In this *novela* Cervantes develops one of his favorite themes, that of the young woman who preserves her *honestidad* in the midst of the traffic of the world, through her own decision rather than external pressure. Costanza is a passive character who does not speak, manifest her feelings, or act with the decision and firm will which Preciosa shows. She accords with the ideal imposed by her society, the virtuous and submissive maiden who barely dares look at a man, speaks only when questioned, and always conforms to her parents' will, especially in the choice of a husband. Costanza's embodiment of this ideal is emphasized by her exaggerated *recato* in contrast to her surroundings. Serving as a foil to her are la Arguëllo and la Gellega, who correspond to the traditional literary type of monstrous ugliness and immoral customs, which relates them to Maritornes of the *Quixote*. The treatment of these two perfect antiheroines is burlesque, especially in the case of la Argüello, but Cervantes's portrayal of even the most vile persons always includes a note of comprehension and compassion, and this case is no exception.

35 Bataillon, Marcel. "'La picaresca': A propos de *La pícara Justina*." *Wort und Text*, pp. 233-50.

Justina is not simply the portrait of a real type of *campesina desenvuelta*, infected by loose-living women of the Court. She is a *pícara* who is a living challenge to the *honra* maintained by Spaniards obsessed by *hidalguía*. Through his heroine, López de Ubeda mocks in several veiled ways certain preoccupations and customs related to the concept of *honra*.

36 _____. *Pícaros y picarescas: La pícara Justina*. Madrid: Taurus, 1969. See pp. 175-99.

The above-mentioned pages contain a Spanish translation of the study included in *Wort und Text*.

37 Bauer, Roger. "Les métamorphoses de Diane." *Wort und Text*, pp. 294-314.

In *El desdén con el desdén* Moreto is not striving for immediate psychological verisimilitude; his art is one of allusion to the poetic universe. Diana is comparable to Angelica of Ariosto's *Orlando furioso*, Silvia of Tasso's *Aminta*, various women or nymphs of mythology who refused their lovers, and even the sirens.

Diana is not a *virago* type such as is found in Lope but rather a *grande dame*. Her objections with regard to love are based on a sincere belief, founded in turn on deep feelings. Whereas in Lope the woman whose head is turned by too much reading is a subject of comedy, Diana is a genuine devotee of philosophy. Hers is not borrowed discontent, but has its source in authentic anguish, her reading being a search for the justification of her own attitudes.

*38 Berretini, Célia. "Perfis femininos no teatro de Lope de Vega." O Estado de Sao Paulo, Suplemento Literário, 4 (February 1967), 5.

39 Blue, William R. "Dualities in Calderón's Eco y Narciso." RHM, 39, no. 3 (1976-77), 109-18.

Blue remarks in passing that Liríope is not so one-dimensional as Hesse suggests (see entry 153), when he casts her in the role of antagonist to the love between Eco and Narciso. Besides being the "terrible mother," she is the loving, protective mother.

40 _____. "The Function of the 'Molinera' in Don Gil de las calzas verdes." BCom, 25 (Spring 1973), 14-18.

The song which begins "Al molino del amor / alegre la niña va" offers among other things an insight into the energetic mind of Tirso's protagonist Juana at an important juncture in the play's development. We can see her progress from being confused upon first seeing Martín, to creating confusion for her own purposes and achieving a growing sense of control over herself and others.

41 Bomli, Dr. P. W. La femme dans l'Espagne du Siècle d'Or. The Hague: Martinus Nijhoff, 1950.

Bomli uses many literary sources in his attempt to trace the life of Spanish women in the Golden Age. He discusses in detail various social classes of women; different states of life or domestic roles for women, such as wife and mother, young unmarried woman, nun, dueña, and maid; and "low" types like the pícara, gypsy, courtesan, and procuress. There are also interesting sections on women's customs, feminism, and préciosité. The author observes that women generally appear as adolescents, with a great variety of nuances, but nearly always overcome the obstacles which prevent their marriage to the men they love; that once married, the woman ceases to interest except when a writer needs her to portray certain moral problems; and that the mother figure is only evoked in ridiculous or disagreeable aspects. Women of royalty or nobility and women of easy virtue are familiar figures, but portrayals of the old and poor, the middle class, and the laboring woman are rare or very unrealistic.

Bourland

In sixteenth-century literature the line of conduct traced by Luis de León's La perfecta casada (in which woman is restricted to the home) is adopted as the general rule, but the idea that it is woman herself, and not her surroundings, who acts as the main guardian of her honor infiltrates gradually, marking a forward step regarding the moral value attributed to women. The question of feminism, in the strict sense of the word, becomes very important in seventeenth-century literature, all the great writers except Quevedo being more or less feminists. The right of a young woman to freely choose her life companion is unanimously recognized. While she is not permitted to become a bluestocking, a woman is allowed to develop her mind, the ignorant woman being presented as possessing no charm. However, the writers are feminist only to a degree, for they see as the only final solution to the feminist problem the woman's return to domestic duties and sacrifice, provided it be on a reasonable basis; i.e., a marriage freely chosen. Two feminist figures preferable to others because of the moderation of their views are Calderón's Clara of Mañanas de abril y mayo and Eugenia of Guárdate del agua mansa.

42 Bourland, Caroline B. "Aspectos de la vida del hogar en el siglo XVII según las novelas de D.ª Mariana de Carabajal y Saavedra." Homenaje ofrecido a Menéndez Pidal. Vol. 2. Madrid: Hernando, 1925, pp. 331-68.

In novelas such as Carabajal's we get a truer and more complete picture of the family than in the theater of the period. For example, rather than force a husband on an unwilling daughter, the father often yields to her wishes and at times is reluctant for her to marry at all, wanting to keep her near him. Brothers, instead of being suspicious guardians of their sisters, are frequently united to them in great love and trust. Carabajal gives us portraits of widows who are competent and energetic and also some interesting and believable relationships between mother and daughter. Her characters are drawn mainly from the lesser nobility and upper middle class.

43 Brancaforte, Benito. "El mágico prodigioso and St. Augustine's Confessions." Estudios de literatura española ofrecidos a Marcos A. Morínigo. Madrid: Insula, 1971, pp. 19-35.

Calderón's Justina is comparable to Monica, mother of St. Augustine, in her disinterested love for Cyprian and strong desire for his conversion and salvation. She has both a negative and a positive role; to show dramatically the devil's lack of power and to serve as living witness to the work of grace. She is the key to Cyprian's fate, her function being, even more clearly than in the case of Rosaura in La vida es sueño, to lead Cyprian from the cavern of his passions to the light of Christian truth.

44 Bravo-Villasante, Carmen. La mujer vestida de hombre en el teatro español (siglos XVI-XVII). Madrid: Revista de Occidente, 1955.

Around the middle of the sixteenth century there appears in the Spanish theater and novela, with Lope de Rueda's Los engañados and Colloquio de Tymbria and Montemayor's Diana, the type of the woman disguised as a man. The theme, whose origin is most probably not Spanish reality but literature, particularly Italian, proves extremely popular, the two most representative variations in Spanish literature being the mujer enamorada and the heroica guerrera who disdains love and flees men. Lope de Vega, synthesizing the different influences and introducing his own variations, which will become clichés in later dramatists, incorporates the type into the comedia. Lope's school uses the theme abundantly and with great variety. A characteristic of Tirsean plays which employ the theme is the confusion resulting from the multiple disguises used by the female protagonist. Calderón, who creates many virile women, offers relatively few but interesting examples of the disguise theme. It reaches its maximum complication in him, with the simultaneous presentation of a woman dressed as a man and a man disguised as a woman. In the dramatists of Calderón's school we see the degeneration of the theme, with the emphasis on the extravagant, the aberrant, and the pathological.

Bravo-Villasante includes an appendix listing thirteen basic motives, many with subdivisions, for the use of the male disguise. There is also a list of the specific disguises used in various plays.

45 Bruerton, Courtney. "La Ninfa del cielo, La serrana de la Vera, and Related Plays." Estudios hispánicos, pp. 61-97.

La Ninfa del cielo, probably written in collaboration by Vélez de Guevara and Tirso de Molina, if not by the former alone, constitutes one link in the chain of comedias de bandoleras, in which the heroine, to avenge an affront, becomes a bandit and wreaks sanguinary vengeance on the men she encounters; and comedias de bandoleros, wherein the hero, in despair of salvation, turns to a life of crime. Among the other members of the series discussed by Bruerton are Lope's La serrana de la Vera and Las dos bandoleras y Santa Hermandad de Toledo, Mira de Amescua's El esclavo del demonio, and Velez' La serrana de la Vera.

The *comedias de bandoleras* derive from an old ballad theme but give a more humane touch to the original vindictive *serranas*. In the earlier plays we observe the anti-heroines--who act contrary to all the traditional qualities of their sex, although they are usually cruel only to men--mainly in their commission of acts of robbery and murder, but in later plays their repentance and conversion takes on increasing importance.

46 Bryans, J. V. "Rosaura Liberated, or A Woman's Rebellion: A New Reading of the Subplot of *La vida es sueño*." *University of British Columbia Hispanic Studies*. Edited by Harold Livermore. London: Tamesis Books, 1974, pp. 19-32.

The play is, among other things, a kind of obstacle course for Rosaura, the most important difficulties being those created by the rules of honor which governed a woman's conduct. Rosaura is an independent spirit, capable of deciding for herself how far in any given situation she must accept or reject society's norms. Her independence should not be exaggerated, however, since she chooses to disregard conventions and adopt a male role only when a difficult situation makes this choice inevitable, and she is clearly willing to return to a more properly feminine and passive role when possible. She has a strong sense of personal integrity and an unswerving commitment to her own honor. Nevertheless, Calderón does not present Rosaura's actions in an entirely favorable light. By means of the many parallels between her and Segismundo, he seems to contrast the prince's final victory over his passion for vengeance with Rosaura's passionate and anarchic regard for worldly honor, in order to show the superiority of Segismundo's conception.

47 Burke, James F. "The *Estrella de Sevilla* and the Tradition of Saturnine Melancholy." *BHS*, 51 (April 1974), 137-56.

Estrella is identified, in the astrological symbolism of the play, with Saturn. In accord with the Aristotelian tradition of saturnine melancholy, she is the catalyst which reactivates in the king the awareness of his proper role, leading him to control his passions. Since Saturn is ambivalent, however, Estrella has a negative influence on Busto and Sancho Ortiz.

48 Canamis, George. "El hondo simbolismo de 'La hija de Agi Morato'." *CHA*, no. 319 (January 1977), pp. 71-102.

When she first arrives at the inn with the Captive, Cervantes's Zoraida symbolizes the Virgin Mary. When the Captive begins his tale, however, she becomes a symbol of Christ the Redeemer. In rescuing him from the hell of

Algiers, she is a figure of the Savior who redeems mankind from Satan's captivity.

49 Cañedo, Jesús. "Tres pícaros, el amor y la mujer." Ibero, 1 (1969), 193-227.
Although Cañedo's study focuses more on the attitude toward women of Lázaro, Alemán's Guzmán, and Quevedo's Pablos than on the female characters themselves, he does point out the great influence of the mother in all three cases. Women for these pícaros are primarily a means to material advantages as well as instruments for the satisfaction of their concupiscence.

50 Caro Baroja, Julio. Las brujas y su mundo. Madrid: Revista de Occidente, 1961.
The author discusses very briefly the theme of witches in Golden Age literature. In "realistic" works such as Cervantes's El coloquio de los perros, Quevedo's El Buscón, and Vélez de Guevara's El diablo cojuelo, the witch becomes simply one more type of character in a varied world, and any condemnation of her actions plays a very secondary part. By using humor in small but effective doses, these writers make people see that witchcraft is an absurdity.

51 _____. "¿Es de origen mítico la 'leyenda' de la Serrana de la Vera?" Revista de Dialectología y Tradiciones Populares, 2 (1946), 568-72.
Examination of the romances, some from the sixteenth and seventeenth centuries, and of the oral tradition related to the Serrana de la Vera produces the following list of characteristics on the part of the protagonist: she is a wild woman, a huntress, who lives in a mountain cave or grotto; she is very beautiful, with blonde hair, dark eyes, and fair skin; she has a virile and cruel character; she seduces every man she encounters and, after sexual intercourse, kills him by throwing him off a precipice. The author concludes that the theme is the last avatar of an ancient mountain divinity.

52 Casa, Frank P. "Diana's Challenge in El desdén con el desdén." RJ, 23 (1972), 307-18.
By rejecting love, Diana threatens to upset the balance in her kingdom and to deny her own destiny as queen and as a member of society. Educated beyond what Moreto considers her need, she misinterprets the function of knowledge by challenging the structure of society. The extreme nature of her opinion holds within it the seeds of its own destruction, but a catalyst is necessary to set off the reaction. Her

fall is not seen as the punishment of a disturbing element but as the joyful reintegration of an indispensable member into society.

Diana's rejection of love is based not on indifference to that sentiment but on a very high conception, and perhaps fear, of the responsibility it entails. She understands love as a total surrender of the self, and this she cannot tolerate. There is in the stated but undeveloped Diana motif a residue of the struggle of women to maintain their independence from men. There is also in Diana a hint of the man-devourer. Her position assumes the proportions of a revenge against men in general and is therefore destructive. It may also be interpreted as an entertaining game for a woman who is insistently pressed.

53 _____. "Honor and the Wife-Killers of Calderón." BCom, 29 (Spring 1977), 6-23.

In the three plays El médico de su honra, A secreto agravio, secreta venganza, and El Pintor de su deshonra, the choice open to the wife is severely restricted: either a return to her lover with the concomitant destruction of her social and moral self, or a rejection of the lover with its implications of victory over self, retention of self-esteem, and the sacrifice of a dormant love. Neither Mencía, Leonor, or Serafina is observed in the act of consciously choosing one direction or the other, a pattern which indicates the author's marginal interest in the woman's dilemma and greater concern for the husband's reaction. Still, the women fail the test of their honor and so must eventually be judged. The increasing guilt of the wife from the first to the last play is reflected in the different deaths meted out to them.

54 Casalduero, Joaquín. "La Galatea." Suma cervantina. Edited by J. B. Avalle-Arce and E. C. Riley. London: Tamesis Books, Limited, 1973, pp. 27-46.

In Cervantes's novel it is not Galatea but Gelasia--disdainful beauty, a being very close to pagan nature--who most resembles the mythological figure over whom Polyphemus anguished. Cervantes humanizes Galatea by having her act in a social and moral milieu, and like Dorotea, Zoraida, Sigismunda, and the heroines of so many novelas ejemplares, Galatea suffers.

55 _____. "Guillén de Castro: Primera comedia de Las mocedades del Cid." Estudios sobre el teatro español. Second Edition. Madrid: Gredos, 1967. See especially pp. 85-88.

The author contrasts Urraca and Jimena in their love for

Rodrigo. Whereas Urraca is totally satisfied by Rodrigo's presence and directs her passion, in which eroticism is without doubt the dominant factor, toward him, Jimena withdraws more into her own center when he is present. She is absorbed by a spiritual attraction, the sexual being relegated to the most hidden and subconscious level of her being. Her eroticism erupts, however, in the *romance* of the third act, revealing her delicacy, femininity, and youthful inexperience.

56 _____. *Sentido y forma de las Novelas ejemplares*. Second Edition. Madrid: Gredos, 1969.

The passion of the Baroque woman replaces the contentment of her Renaissance counterpart. Baroque feminine beauty is dark, in contrast to the blonde hair and clear eyes of the Renaissance, but the latter tradition persists through Quevedo.

Casalduero provides insights into the character and function of many individual heroines of the *novelas*. Preciosa of *La gitanilla* incarnates the moral ideal of the feminine in the Counter Reformation. Cervantes avoids making her profound sense of *honestidad* become prudishness by insisting also on her *desenvoltura*. Leonisa of *El amante liberal* reveals Cervantes's conception of purity as a virtue dedicated to marriage and fruitful maternity. Leonora of *El celoso extremeño* is the one exception among these heroines to the ideal woman of the early Baroque. There is no active principle in her for either good or evil. The strong sexuality of all the female servants is a kind of orchestral background to the discovery of the sexual in Leonora. Costanza of *La ilustre fregona* is a striking contrast to Leonora. Whereas the latter, precisely because of her separation from the world, is incapable of offering the least resistance to the enemy of virtue, Costanza, who lives uninterruptedly subject to danger and in constant relation to men, emerges victorious from all attacks because of her inherent *honestidad*. The two heroines of *Las dos doncellas*--of whom Leocadia seems to be simply a duplicate of Teodosia, with only those variations necessary for plot movement--are neither ideal norms of conduct nor slaves of instinct but simply human. In them, Cervantes collaborates in the creation of the socially heroic type of woman, who will crystallize in the late Baroque with Rojas. The heroine of *La señora Cornelia* illustrates Cervantes's ability to portray motherhood with extraordinarily seductive delicacy yet without falling into sentimentality. Her physical maternity is filled with spirit.

57 _____. Sentido y forma del Quijote, 1605-1615. Madrid: Ediciones Insula, 1966.

Casalduero comments at different points on several female characters of the Quixote. Marcela is an idealized woman, but one who is the companion of man; she is the cause of a happiness or sorrow strictly human, not a deified being. Dulcinea is not like Marcela; she is an idea, a mujer-quimera. She is Don Zuixote's star and at the same time his guide and inspirer. In Dorotea, Cervantes offers a compendium of the three possible relations between the sexes: self-giving, killing, and flight. Luscinda, with her moral suffering, incarnates the woman of the Counter Reformation. Extremely honesta and beautiful, she must safeguard her virtue in the world, not in an academy or convent. For Cervantes only the free woman can be honesta, not with the freedom of the pastoral fields but with the possibility of exercising her will in choice. Zoraida represents the moral experience of captivity, the beauty of faith and hope in the midst of all the sorrow and ugliness of life. She is to the Captive what Dulcinea is to Don Quixote. Clara is the pure and brilliant star which guides man. She is the opposite of Marcela in that we contemplate in her, innocence and the birth of love in a real medium, the urban. Altisidora is one of those young women who aspire to marriage; therefore any departure from honestidad will lead her not to passion or sensuality but to frivolity. Maritornes is a figure of carnal love; a grotesque vision of the idea of corporeal beauty without virtue.

58 Case, Thomas E. "El papel de Inés en Peribáñez." Duquesne Hispanic Review, 10 (1971), 1-9. Also in RF, 84 (1972), 546-52.

The character Inés is understandable only as part of the psychology of Casilda. Together they represent the virtues and faults of woman, Inés's weakness and lack of scruples contrasting vividly with the protagonist's integrity. Lope finds in Inés an efficacious means to carry out the designs of Luján and the Comendador without risking Casilda's virtue.

59 Casona, Alejandro. "La doncella galán." Nov (18 August 1958).

The adoption by the female of the male disguise is a theatrical device at least as old as Aristophanes. The tradition in Spain can be traced back to the popular romances, such as the memorable "La doncella guerrera," the most illustrious example in the Spanish classical theater being Rosaura of Calderón's La vida es sueño. The incident in Chapter Forty-nine of the Quixote in which Cervantes pokes fun at the young woman dressed in green who has left home in male disguise in order to see the world, is a clear allusion to Tirso's *Don Gil de las calzas verdes*.

*60 _____. "Las mujeres de Lope de Vega." *Escuelas de España*. Vol. 2. Madrid: n.p., 1935, pp. 194-208.

61 _____. "El secreto de Dulcinea." *Nov* (January 4, 1959).
Dulcinea is simply the feminine projection of Don Quixote's own soul.

62 _____. "Tres mujeres en la vida de Lope." *Cuadernos de Bellas Artes*, México, 3, no. 11 (1962), 56-64.
Beneath the garb of Lope's feminine artistic creations, it is not difficult to discover the women of flesh and blood who inspired them. The pale and melancholy "Marfisa" of *La Dorotea* is his cousin María de Aragón, whom he recalls with a tenderness full of contrition. "Belisa," or his first wife Isabel de Urbina, is presented in one famous poem as a dramatically tragic figure, a new Medea, though she was in reality a quite different personality; serene and genteel, with a beauty marked by white skin and black hair. The authentic outlines of "Lucinda," or the actress Micaela de Luján, the great romantic passion of Lope's plenitude, escape us under an avalanche of idealizing metaphors. The only authentic detail we can capture is her blue eyes.

63 Castro, Américo. *El pensamiento de Cervantes*. Madrid: Hernando, 1925. See pp. 126-27, n. 1.
Cervantes has created enchanting feminine types but given very unfavorable opinions on woman's character. Since opinions cannot be found in his writing to oppose these negative evaluations, one must conclude that Cervantes did not esteem women when he analyzed them critically. All this corresponds to his double vision of the poetic universal and the prosaic particular.

64 Castro, Carmen. "En el año internacional de la mujer." *EstLit*, no. 567 (1 July 1975), pp. 4-7.
When Cervantes wrote the *Quixote*, he had already created a free feminine character, Gelasia of *La Galatea*, but Marcela is more; she is a free and personal feminine attitude. Much more than a "no" to Grisóstomo's love, she is a "yes" to a life freely chosen by her. She does not appear in order to form part of a pastoral-student scene but to defend the integral liberty of the human person.

65 _____. "Personajes femeninos de Cervantes: Las mujeres del *Quijote*." *ACer*, 3 (1953), 43-85.
Castro discusses thirty or more female figures in the

Quixote. Among them are the housekeeper and niece, women who are neither attractive nor interesting but are needed in order to detach Don Quixote from his immediate environment. Dulcinea has two missions: to make Don Quixote emerge as normal, complete, and firm in a human dimension through his love for her, and to contrast with the other women. Marcela, integral and self-enclosed, is a diamond for whom Cervantes is concerned to provide an appropriate setting. Luscinda is a foil for Dorotea, who is the feminine character most important to Cervantes. Although the same conventional elements are used to describe their beauty and perfection, the two do not otherwise resemble each other. Luscinda is the woman for whom love is the only possibility in life; in Dorotea there is also friendship. Luscinda is perfect as amada; Dorotea, as a woman, because she is a whole woman. Dorotea is the only female character comparable to both Don Quixote and Sancho in the fullness with which she has been created.

66 Cauz, Francisco A. "Salas Barbadillo y La Celestina." Boletín Cultural y Bibliográfico, 14, no. 3 (1971), 104-108.
In La hija de Celestina, Elena's mother, supposedly a second Celestina, does not play an active role in the work, and Elena herself has essentially nothing in common with either Melibea or Celestina. The celestinesque characters in "La madre" and La escuela de Celestina are closely linked to the development of the action but are mere shadows of their prototype.

67 Cirurgião, Antonio A. "O papel da beleza na Diana de Jorge de Montemor." Hispania, 51 (September 1968), 402-407.
The fundamental quality of woman in the Diana is beauty. Beauty is what defines woman and gives her the greatest value. Feminine beauty in the Diana has more of a substantial than an accidental character and is thus considered more in its abstract, metaphysical aspect than in its concrete, physical one. Woman, being essentially beautiful, is essentially lovable. Montemayor sees in woman, more than anything else, the object of cult and veneration. His mission, which is common to almost all Renaissance writers and artists, is to exalt woman as the most beautiful creature on earth and therefore the most worthy of being loved and sung.

68 Claros, Eufemiano. "La Dulcinea del Toboso." Honduras Rotaria, Tegucigalpa, Honduras, 5, no. 27 (December 1947), 10, 14.
Cervantes exercises his talent most exquisitely in his portrayal of women. In Dulcinea, ideal incarnation of Don Quixote's dreams, Cervantes synthesizes all feminine charms.

69 Clavería, Carlos. "Gustavo Adolfo y Cristina de Suecia, vistos por los españoles de su tiempo: II." *Clavileño*, 3, no. 18 (1952), 17-27.

Whereas Part I of this study dealt mainly with Gustavo Adolfo, Part II concentrates on his daughter. Among the literary works which treat Cristina are popular poetic compositions born of enthusiastic fervor at her conversion. The great Spanish poet of Cristina's conversion was Bernardino de Rebolledo, in whose *La constancia victoriosa: Egloga sacra* there are two poems addressed to her, one being a sketch of the Swedish queen. She is also the protagonist of two works by Calderón, the *comedia*, *Afectos de odio y amor* and the *auto sacramental*, *La protestación de la Fe*. In the former, the interpretation of the figure is conventionally arbitrary, the product of the poet's fantasy, though there are passages where one glimpses the qualities of the real Cristina. The protagonist of the *auto* is a warrior who despoils herself of her arms and gives herself over to books, renouncing her errors and converting to obedience to the Church.

70 Clements, Robert J., and Joseph Gibaldi. *Anatomy of the Novella: The European Tale Collection from Boccaccio and Chaucer to Cervantes*. New York: New York University Press, 1977. See especially Ch. VII.

Spanish authors mentioned include Cervantes, Tirso de Molina, and María de Zayas. Estefanía of Cervantes's *El casamiento engañoso* is an example of the deceptive and scheming female. The same author's *El celoso extremeño* gives a unique twist to the endless *novella* theme of the attempt to keep a wife faithful and chaste.

Tirso finds it easy to sympathize with female characters treated as chattel and used to further the financial and social aspirations of their households. His *comedia El burlador de Sevilla* could be viewed as a tract on the abuse of women during the Golden Age. The *novella Los tres maridos burlados* surprisingly takes a stand for justifiable divorce.

María de Zayas is a militant feminist whose major theme in the *Novelas amorosas y ejemplares* is that women are oppressed and men are the oppressors. Through writers like Zayas, women gradually metamorphosed the once predominantly misogynistic genre into a vehicle for propounding their own strongly feminist ideas.

71 Colón, Isabel. "María de Zayas y Sotomayor: Algo más que una pesimista (sic) en el siglo XVII." *EstLit*, no. 633 (1 April 1978), pp. 17-18.

We cannot reduce Zayas's intent to the defense of woman.

The Baroque theme of the deceitfulness of life is basic in her novelas; man's deceitfulness toward woman being one more element within a general corruption and also its cause. The woman who has placed the meaning of her existence in human love or marriage must be undeceived, and when she is, the only refuge is the convent.

72 Cornil, Suzanne. Inès de Castro: Contribution à l'étude du développement littéraire du thème dans les littératures romanes. Brussels: Palais des Academies, 1952. See pp. 54-82.
Cornil deals with various Portuguese and Spanish works on the Inés de Castro theme. If don Pedro is the hero of the chronicle, it is Inés who lives in the memory and imagination of the following generations. The best dramatic interpretation of the theme in Spanish literature is Luis Vélez de Guevara's Reinar después de morir. However, Inés, like most of the characters, is, as it were, paralyzed by historic tradition, being above all very beautiful and very dignified. The most interesting character from the theatrical point of view, and one who is entirely original, is Blanca.

73 Cossío, José María. "Notas al romancero: Caracteres populares de la feminidad en 'La doncella que va a la guerra'." Escorial, 6, no. 17 (1942), 413-23.
In this romance popular sensibility confronts a most delicate theme: the qualities or character of femininity. All the signs of the young woman's sex which are foreseen as possibly revealing her identity are able to be disguised, but other indicators are of an origin so purely feminine they cannot be hidden. Some of these are physiological, others emotional. The various tests to which the disguised young woman is subjected are proposed by the mother of the prince but are based on the keen observation of feminine habits or characteristics as rural sagacity understands them.

74 Cotarelo y Valledor, Armando. La belleza femenina en las obras de Cervantes. Santiago, Chile: Impr. de "El Eco", 1905.
For Cervantes the most perfect natural beauty is that of a beautiful woman. He follows the mode in portraying ideal feminine beauty. For example, all his heroines are more or less blonde, and in the case of those who would not be so naturally because of their race, he does not mention hair color. Like his contemporaries, he opts for green or hazel eyes, small mouth, red lips, small white teeth, flexible waist, and small feet. He gives many examples of

adherence to the opinion that it is elegant for a woman to dress ornately to enhance her beauty. Yet above all these natural and artificial beauties he ranks spiritual beauty, born of chastity, modesty, good habits, and virtue.

75 _____. *La Dulcinea de Cervantes*. Madrid: Impr. Magisterio Español, 1947.

This study is virtually the same as the author's *La belleza femenina en las obras de Cervantes*, Dulcinea being a compendium of all the qualities discussed in the earlier work.

76 Crabtree, Mary Frances. "El parentesco de *Reinar después de morir* de Luis Vélez de Guevara y *La Reine Morte* de Henry de Montherlant: Una comparación." *Hispano*, no. 65 (January 1979), pp. 59-67.

The greatest similarity between the two plays with respect to the characters is in regard to the Infanta. In both she is antithetical to Inés. Whereas Inés represents beauty, is associated with a gentle bird, and aspires to love; the Infanta represents *grandeza*, is associated with a rapacious bird, and aspires to reign. Other aspects of Inés's character and function in the Spanish play are seen more clearly when compared with the French drama. In the former, Inés dies a victim of *razón de estado*; in the latter, of an aging king who wants to prove he can still act vigorously. In the Spanish work Inés is a protagonist together with the Prince, while in the French play her role is essential only when she serves as audience to the king's confession. In both plays Inés reigns in two senses: figuratively, through the law of God, she has power over death, over every earthly difficulty and pettiness; literally, she reigns in the heart of the Prince and the people.

77 Criado de Val, M. "Melibea y Celestina ante el juicio de Don Quijote." *ACer*, 4 (1954), 187-98.

Cervantes's feminine protagonists always bear a literary stamp because he lacked an interesting, living model. He was very fond of the type of woman who is almost a child and who lives a secluded life, but in whom there lies hidden a capacity for decision and an independent spirit. His feminine characters of this type are modest disciples of Melibea. In fact, Cervantes breaks up Rojas's character Melibea into a multitude of secondary figures, almost always conventional, representatives of an idea or a moral problem. The consistently unfortunate intervention of the parents is a habitual theme with regard to the feminine protagonists of *Don Quixote*. Cervantes fixes the responsibility for the passing infection represented by Celestina in the inevitable hypocrisy of social life.

78 Cro, Stelio. "Cervantes entre Don Quijote y Dulcinea." Hispano, no. 47 (January 1973), pp. 47-57.

In the conception of the character Dulcinea, Cervantes had in mind the parody of the dama of the knights errant; in her evolution he gave form to a profound intuition of the unattainable ideal. Dulcinea acquires greater importance in the second part of the Quixote, in which Don Quixote and Sancho collaborate in her creation. This part presents a tension between the knight and Dulcinea, which becomes the axis of the novel. Dulcinea is a modern character in the sense that she lays bare the psychological complexity of man, assaulted by opposing tendencies: feeling and reason, fantasy and reality, subject and object. Dulcinea, an ideal creature, ardently loved and progressively dissolved in a game of ambiguous dialectics which corresponds to the process of the hidalgo's recovery of sanity, could be the symbol of the Quixote's supreme disinterestedness.

79 Cubeñas, José Antonio. "Análisis de Fuenteovejuna de Lope de Vega." Abside, 40 (1976), 297-307.

Laurencia, one of the two main characters around which the play's action is polarized, personifies the sentiments and attitudes of the populace, and the consciousness of their rights on the part of the new autonomous and democratic communities which were everywhere arising and supplanting the old order. Her personal valor, her decision and initiative, entail no loss of femininity.

80 Chacón y Calvo, José María. "De Pedro de Urdemalas a La gitanilla." DMar (12 October 1947), p. 35.

Preciosa, heroine of La gitanilla, is one of the immortal types created by Cervantes. Bélica of Pedro de Urdemalas, who is beautiful and discreet and who from the beginning seems more like a señora than a gypsy girl, is very similar to Preciosa, but she does not attain to such an ideal signification.

81 _____. "El realismo ideal de La gitanilla." BACL, 2 (1953), 246-67.

Cervantes's Preciosa belongs to the lineage of ideal creatures who purify all that surrounds them, and inspire in all the desire for goodness and beauty. She belongs to the same family as Dulcinea, but more than a symbol she is a surprising creature, ideal yet full of reality, and worthy of belonging to the race of symbols.

82 Damiani, Bruno M. "Un aspecto histórico de La lozana andaluza." MLN, 87 (March 1972), 178-92.

Damiani discusses Francisco Delicado's presentation of the "mundo alegre y libertino" of Renaissance courtesans. In his description of the various types of courtesan and of their way of life, he is very faithful to historical reality.

83 _____. "La lozana andaluza: Tradición literaria y sentido moral." Actas del Tercer Congreso, pp. 241-48.

It has been well said that the protagonist of Delicado's novel, beautiful, sensual, and astute, resembles the youthful Celestina. In addition, by reason of her realistic and objective vision of life and her condition as a young and beautiful woman in search of pleasure and gain, Lozana is the only example of a female pícara in the sixteenth century. Damiani mentions Gómez de la Serna's opinion that the novel's moral aim is the depiction of prostitutes as they are, the miserable life they lead in having to deal with repugnant beings, and the material and moral dangers lying in wait for those who have relations with them.

84 D'Antuono, Nancy L. "Discreción as a Remedy against Adverse Fortune: Boccaccio's Third Story of the Third Day and Lope's La discreta enamorada." BCom, 27 (Spring 1975), 26-35.

Lope, unlike Boccaccio, stresses discreta as the epithet for his heroine, relegating industria to only two passages. Since marriage is the goal set for Fenisa, her extraordinary cleverness must be directed to the achievement of this morally acceptable end. Although discreción in women ordinarily meant chastity, modesty, and reserve, Lope uses it here in a different sense. In fact, in five of the eight plots borrowed from Boccaccio, Lope shows a woman to be the strong, energizing force which moves the play to its conclusion, to be equal in stature to the male and thus worthy of the adjective discreta. Discreta and enamorada would seem to be mutually contradictory terms, but Fenisa is distinct from other enamoradas because she has already achieved that discreción ordinarily seen as an effect of love, rather than as its prerequisite. Gerarda and Belisa contrast with the protagonist in this respect by their lack of judiciousness and circumspection.

85 Darst, David H. "The Two Worlds of La ninfa del cielo." HR, 42 (Spring 1974), 209-20.

There are two levels of action in this Tirsean drama, the particular history of Ninfa, Countess of Valdeflor, and the universal blueprint of all sinners who eventually repent and are saved. This last level corresponds to the life of

Mary Magdalene and the four spiritual stages through which she passed, as expounded by Pedro Malón de Chaide in La conversión de la Madalena. With respect to the first level, Ninfa is indeed an extraordinary woman, but love dissolves her Diana-like persona, the mask she wears to cover her vulnerable femininity. When, from the lowest point of her passivity and submission, she reverts with double force to the camouflaging of her wounded femininity behind the masculine persona of the bandolera, she becomes doubly hidden from herself. Carlos's return and pledge of fidelity causes her to drop the bandit mask and become her true feminine self. Her passionate carnal love for Carlos is not the expression of her full nature either, but merely the natural outburst of her potential for a perfect love.

86 David-Peyré, Yvonne. "Lope de Vega ante la mujer enferma." PSA, 61, no. 182 (May 1971), 117-39.
Every young woman in the Golden Age suffered from a malady which was the result of a boring, restricted life. Cervantes gives us the best description of this kind of life in Leonora, protagonist of El celoso extremeño. Lope confronts with astonishing realism the infirmity frequently called opilación, symptoms of which were languor, melancholy, and fatigue. One example is found in El acero de Madrid, where the illness is not real but simply a tactic.

87 Deleito y Piñuela, José. La mujer, la casa y la moda (en la España del Rey Poeta). Third Edition. Madrid: Espasa-Calpe, 1966.
Taking many examples from literature, the author discusses various types of women in the reign of Felipe IV, such as the importunate and capricious, the learned, the ridiculously affected, the tapada; aspects of their lives and character, such as their isolation and childishness, social visits, love trysts and courting rituals; and issues concerning them, such as honor and dishonor. Among the authors discussed are Lope and Tirso, who are more or less realistic in their presentation of women, their character and behavior; Calderón and Alarcón, who idealize women; Cervantes, who shows an understanding attitude toward feminine weakness; and Quevedo, a raging misogynist, whose attitude may perhaps be compared to that of a drunkard who in later years abhors what he had earlier shown an extreme enthusiasm for. What appears to be contempt and rage in Quevedo, however, may possibly be better described as the malice of wit. Very evident in the literature of the time are feelings of anger, scorn, contempt, and rancor toward women, which take shape in a special misogynistic body of writing, culminating in the satirists, costumbristas, and entremesistas.

88 Deneuville, Dominique. Sainte Thérèse d'Avila et la femme. Lyon: Editions du Chalet, 1964. Also Santa Teresa de Jesús y la mujer. Translated by F. Gutiérrez. Barcelona: Herder, 1966.

The author of the preface, Pierre Blanchard, observes that whoever reads Teresa's works is struck by her reflections on woman. Her concept of woman is a very delicate issue, not easy to evaluate. She appears to reveal what could almost be called an inferiority complex, but this is not really the case. Teresa is aware of the mystery which woman is, not only to man but even to herself. Moreover, much of what she says regarding woman must be understood in the light of her sense of humor. For Teresa, woman's limitations are her destin, but the great perspectives which God opens for her in His mercy and which cause her to surpass herself in deeds of magnanimity are her destinée.

Deneuville believes that the basic message of Luis de León's La perfecta casada corresponds to Teresa's thought when she tells her Daughters that if they do what depends on them, God will make them so virile that they will astonish men themselves. She does not wish to alienate her nuns from their true femininity; indeed, she exhorts them to live as true followers of Our Lady and to be servants of love. She does, however, want to preserve them from certain deviations and dangers of femininity: capricious changes of spirit, affectations of sensibility, and illusions of the imagination. The virility she desires for them is that given by the Spirit of God.

89 Díaz-Plaja, Guillermo. "La mujer y el honor en la obra de Tirso de Molina." Nuevo asedio a don Juan. Buenos Aires: Editorial Sudamericana, 1947, pp. 41-55.

The predominance of the woman in Tirso's work takes two contradictory directions; on the one hand, a series of feminine types magnificent in their integrity and dignity, such as María de Molina of La prudencia en la mujer; and on the other, a series of enamored women who use any and all means to achieve their amorous aims. Díaz-Plaja mentions four subgroups of the latter type, identified by Muñoz y Peña: the woman who disguises herself, usually as a man, in order to search for her lover; the dama who falls in love with a man of inferior social rank; the woman who conceals her true feelings in order to achieve her goal; and the woman of humble lineage who falls in love for the first time. The accusation that Tirso presented the women of his time with extraordinary liviandad is beside the point; he was not attempting to reflect contemporary society but to portray fictional entities.

90 Dille, Glen F. "The Comedia Serafina and Its Relationship to La Celestina." Celestinesca, 1, no. 2 (1977), 15-20.

In spite of comic variations introduced by the anonymous author, such as the lack of witchcraft and the elevation of a low class tercera to a dueña honrada, a woman of considerable income and social standing, there is no mistaking the celestinesque origins of Artemia. As the main comic figure, she shows herself to be hypocritical, lewd, and hedonistic. Her downfall results not from greed but hypocrisy, a quality she shares with all the other female characters of the Serafina.

91 Dolan, Kathleen. "Eurydice and the Imagery of Redemption: Calderón's Auto del divino Orfeo." PPNCFL, 26, no. 1 (1975), 196-98.

Dolan discusses the figure of Eurydice as symbolic of human nature, Eve, and the self.

92 Dopico, Blanca. "Las mujeres ejemplares de Cervantes." Universidad de la Habana, 13, nos. 76-81 (1941), 155-86.

Observing that these are by no means great feminine characters, Dopico discusses many of the women from Cervantes's novelas, after identifying them with an abstract concept or phrase which communicates their essence. Leonisa of El amante liberal is Love; Leocadia of La fuerza de la sangre, Maternity. The exemplarity of Preciosa of La gitanilla, or Grace, lies not only in her virtues, especially chastity, but also in her innate sense of poetry. Teodosia and Leocadia of Las dos doncellas, or Honor, are pioneers in the feminist struggle. They are examples of feminine intrepidity in a social milieu which saw women as objects of pleasure or simply servant-companions. Leonora of El celoso extremeño, or Infidelity, is the propitiatory victim of the passions of man. Without ethical or tragic grandeur, she is condemned to purge the sin of infidelity, into which she falls without love or egotism, without willing or even knowing it. Pipota, la Gananciosa, la Cariarta, and la Escalanta of Rinconete y Cortadillo, or the Ignoble Women, are grotesque caricatures of vice, and desolate sketches of a sad reality which drags them to sin through idleness, lust, or greed.

93 Dunn, Peter N. Castillo Solórzano and the Decline of the Spanish Novel. Oxford: Basil Blackwell, 1952. See pp. 54-55.

The heroines of Castillo's novelas, the axis about which all the plot action revolves, are more highly developed as types than the heroes. Highly sexed, their one aim is to marry, but they are often capricious in their choice of a lover. They are susceptible to soft words, songs in their praise, and novelty; they are unpredictable, fickle, and lacking in judgment. The heroine, although generally more passive than her male counterpart, does often take the initiative in the amorous chase. In Los efectos que hace amor the lady actually kidnaps her lover. In spite of this, women in Castillo's novelas are "the weaker sex."

94 _____. "'Materia la mujer, el hombre forma': Notes on the Development of a Lopean Topos." Homenaje a William L. Fichter. Edited by A. David Kossoff and José Amor y Vásquez. Madrid: Editorial Castalia, 1971, pp. 189-99.

Among Lope's plays in which the topos appears are Los locos de Valencia, Los Tellos de Meneses, El sembrar en buena tierra, and Virtud, pobreza y mujer. In the first, the topos is one element in a series of pedantries, enhancing the effect of mock gravity. In the second, Lope varies the original topos, saying woman is matter; man, form. He thus stresses the protection and social identity bestowed by man on woman, as ordained by Nature. In the third play, form is identified with creativity; by submitting to it, matter acquires purpose and a being capable of perfection. Similarly, woman fulfills herself in the service of her husband and thereby acknowledges her place in the family and society. The form provided by society for woman is a discipline which frees her from the constraints of her "unformed" self. In the fourth play, the topos is used to observe that it is essential to the feminine condition to be always asking for something.

95 _____. "A Postscript to La Lozana andaluza: Life and Poetry." RF, 88 (1976), 355-60.

Whereas in the body of the narrative Delicado presents Lozana as a personal acquaintance, in the appendices she becomes, by synecdoche, Rome, the civitas meretrix. Dunn believes that Lozana rewrites her life on the pattern of St. Mary of Egypt, by retiring to an island and becoming a pious recluse.

96 Edwards, Gwynne. "Calderón's La hija del aire and the Classical Type of Tragedy." BHS, 44 (July 1967), 161-94.

In Part I Semíramis is presented as aspiring to a completely worthy end but as possessing a character detrimental to that end. She is convinced she can avoid the predicted disaster through the exercise of reason, but it is obvious her over-passionate nature will make the continued exercise of reason unlikely. Her ambitious aims are not wrong or

Edwards

unnatural in themselves; they become so only when she begins to play off Menón and Nino, using their passion for her as a springboard for her own ends. Her tragedy lies in the hardening of her ambition to such an extent that it becomes ruthless.

As the central tragic figure of Part II, Semíramis acquires a Satanic grandeur. The pity and fear we felt for her in Part I become terror as her ambition converts the happiness and freedom to which she aspired into exercises in tyranny and injustice, until she is eventually destroyed. She attains the stature of a truly great tragic heroine as she is swept to her doom by passions she cannot control.

97 _____. "Calderón's La hija del aire in the Light of His Sources." BHS, 43 (July 1966), 177-96.

Calderón's most immediate source was Cristóbal Virués's La gran Semíramis. Earlier sources do not see her ambition as a motivating factor in Semiramis's rise and fall, but Virués singles it out as the main driving force in her character and the principal source of her downfall. Calderón also shifts the emphasis in the sources. Whereas they couple her beauty with intelligence as the source of her attraction, Calderón focuses on beauty in order to underline the purely physical nature of her hold over men. Where they portray her as both ambitious and lustful, he makes her ambitious to the point of nearly total exclusion of any erotic feeling. He conceives of her as a woman who is spiritually masculine; in fact, abnormal. Nevertheless, he depicts the emergence of her ambition gradually, so she is a more rounded and convincing human being than any of the sources suggest.

98 El Saffar, Ruth. Novel to Romance: A Study of Cervantes's Novelas ejemplares. Baltimore: The Johns Hopkins University Press, 1974.

El Saffar offers some very insightful comments on the heroines of the novelas. Leonora, perhaps the most neglected character in critical commentary on El celoso extremeño, is passive and undefined at the beginning. In order to emerge as a credible character, she must make a fundamental choice of her own, independent of the promptings of either Carrizales or Marialonso. This is what happens in her experience with Loaysa. Preciosa of La gitanilla becomes more than she is simply by acting and talking as if she believed it. There is a simultaneous progress in her interest in Andrés and her self-creation. Costanza of La ilustre fregona, like Preciosa, reveals beneath a rustic appearance the ideal feminine virtues of the dominant class: beauty, intelligence, chastity, and self-reliance. Though she is the reverse image of Preciosa, always representing an attitude of compliance and apparently allowing herself to be controlled by everyone around her, she shares with this other heroine a faith in her superiority which reveals a character of great strength and will. Leocadia of Las dos doncellas functions as an exaggeration of repressed aspects of Teodosia. She has no real claim to a separate identity, being Teodosia's dark shadow, exaggerating the dangers of Teodosia's situation, the baseness of her motives, and the extent of her complicity in the destruction of her own honor. Leocadia externalizes the boldness and aggressiveness which Teodosia needs in order to win back Marco Antonio while at the same time preserving her modesty and passivity. Leonisa of El amante liberal is a character in search of her salvation, who must discover herself to be more than a victim, the passive recipient of the passions of others with no criteria of her own for choice. Isabela of La española inglesa symbolizes perfection in a young lady and thus does not develop in the same way as Preciosa or Costanza. In her confident faith she embodies the serenity and changelessness of the stars.

99 _____. "Tres imáges (sic) claves de lo femenino en el Persiles." RCEH, 3 (Spring 1979), 219-36.

The Persiles is distinct from Cervantes's earlier long novels in its presentation of the feminine as an active force, woman as more than a mere reflection of erotic confusions of man, or an object to be obtained and guarded. Although Periandro and Auristela share a central position in the novel, the main problem explored is the effort of the masculine consciousness to integrate itself with the unconscious. While it is true that in La Galatea Cervantes made a great effort to present a feminine as well as a masculine point of view, and that his broad perspective never permitted him to identify with his male characters at the expense of the female ones, still, close analysis of his first works reveals a limitation in his representation of woman, which approaches the stereotypical. The limitation is manifested precisely in the absence of women as mothers. Persiles's journey includes the feminine not only because it introduces his travel companion and alter ego in the figure of a woman, but because the journey itself is organized by a woman, who is mother and queen. The feminine in its role as mother initiates the action which leads to union, in contrast to the masculine, which is represented in its martial, destructive, and divisive aspect.

The stories interpolated between the fifth and tenth chapters of the Persiles, and narrated by men, provide a commentary on the relationship between man and woman which is reflected also in the main characters. In all cases it is the relationship of the man with the woman which determines the successful or unsuccessful outcome of the story. Both Rutilio and Manuel Sosa de Coitiño have created woman to their own image. In the first case, she is progressively degraded from an indiscreet young girl to a sorceress, to a wolf; the external projections which result from man's fear of the voluptuous woman he bears within himself. The second case, the idealization of the woman as something worthy of veneration, is also the result of an incapacity to confront the feminine as something living and independent of the ego's control. The fear in both cases originates in a separation of the material and spiritual such that woman, as a representation of man's soul or essential being, is conceived by the man as too vile or too lofty. The problem is resolved by the juxtaposition of the material and spiritual, symbolized in Periandro by his remaining physically at Auristela's side in the role of brother. This puts an end to the imbalance of angel/demon and situates man and woman on a plane of equality before the Creator. It also replaces the perspective of the ego with the broader one of the inner self, where man and woman coexist as companions in the enterprise of creation.

100 Entrambasaguas, Joaquín de. "Espejo para la mujer en el Renacimiento español." RL, 18, nos. 35-36 (1960), 83-116.

Entrambasaguas treats Juan Luis Vives's concept of the feminine ideal as expressed in De Institutione Feminae Christianae, and its relationship to other works of the sixteenth century, especially those of Antonio de Guevara and Luis de León. Guevara perceives the same problems and gives analogous solutions independently and simultaneously. He reveals his conception of the feminine ideal in some of the Epístolas familiares, without approaching the complete systematization of Vives. Luis de León is a passionate follower of Vives and faithfully reproduces the concept which the latter formed of the perfect Spanish woman, separating it from Vives's pedagogical technique. Some of the points on which the three writers harmonize are that a woman must be peaceful, long-suffering, and modest in speech and dress; chastity must be her most essential virtue; she should live a secluded life and occupy herself in domestic tasks; she should know how to conserve what her husband garners; and she must practice active charity toward the needy. In the seventeenth century the canon created by Vives is obliterated in the feminine image of the theater, decadent in a moral and Christian sense.

101 Errázuriz, Helena. "La mujer en tiempos de Fray Luis de León." *CA*, 35 (March-April 1976), 153-60.

Eminently conservative in its focus, Fray Luis de León's *La perfecta casada* addresses only women of the upper class, and even then, fails to touch the soul. He identifies a woman's place as the home; her intellectual status, as one of inferiority to men. He presents the family as a feudal institution, in which the wife is related to the husband as a vassal to his lord. Since she is a sinner and the origin of sin, woman must make expiation and try to perfect herself. The first way a married woman does this is by making her husband confident and secure. It is essential for Fray Luis that a woman be, in order of importance, virginal, neat and clean, a good administrator of the household, and silent. The didactic aspect of the work assumes a satiric *costumbrismo* when the author depicts the faults and vanities of women.

102 Espina, Antonio. "Quevedo y las mujeres." *RdA*, 10 (1947), 349-51.

Although classical Spanish writers generally tend to be harsh with women, it is hard to find any serious writer who equals Quevedo's hostility, his malevolence toward them being much greater than that shown toward his other favorite targets. His attacks against women are not passionate but cold. He even attacks a female saint, Teresa of Avila, protesting the idea of giving her instead of Santiago the honor of being patron of Spain, since he considers it insufferable that even *de tejas arriba* men should have to submit to feminine rule.

103 Espina, Concha. "El feminismo de Cervantes." *DMar* (15 February 1948), p. 36.

In Cervantes's portrayal of women, reality and fantasy, strength and weakness coincide. Although there is a rich variety among them, feeling predominates in all. Cervantes lavished more care and affection on the noblest, however, whose intelligence and courage equal their tenderness and *gracia*. The fact that some of his female figures are vague and conventional may be due partly to the taste of the period but also to Cervantes's lack of direct contact with worthy women. Only his genius and tenderness made it possible for him to model the fine and idealistic figures which he did.

104 _____. "Las mujeres del *Quijote*." *Obras completas*. Second Edition. Vol. 2. Madrid: Ediciones Fax, 1955, pp. 826-52.

Cervantes's tolerance and tenderness are refined and augmented when he portrays women. He created one of the most varied feminine portrait galleries of Spanish art, restoring a sane and reasonable concept of woman.

Espina gives a series of portraits of women from the Quixote, attempting to evoke some aspect of their moral countenance. For example, Aldonza Lorenzo and Dulcinea del Toboso, though they seem contradictory, are really aspects of the same concept, the ideal and real Woman, eternal Woman. Dorotea is a woman who knew how to love, suffer, and sympathize deeply, to cultivate in the honeycomb of her soul the honey of a dream and the wax of sacrifice. Zoraida is a rose of passion and tenderness, with the subtle and complex heart of both the child and the woman. The Duchess, chaste and gentil, valiant, a lover of mountain and river, field and sky, is comparable to Diana the huntress. Teresa Panza possesses the virtues of the race, as well as very human ambitions. The housekeeper and niece, "violetas de paz," pass through the novel like symbols of fidelity, the perfume of modesty.

*105 _____. "Violetas de la paz y de la muerte." La Prensa, New York (16 June and 30 July 1946).

Could not be located but seems to be an extract from the author's "Las mujeres del Quijote."

106 Espresati, Carlos G. Una biografía de Aldonza Lorenzo. Castellón: Hijos de F. Armengot, 1947. Also in Boletín de la Sociedad Castellonense de Cultura (1947), pp. 407-27.

Although basically an imaginative work called Tragicomedia de Aldonza Lorenzo, Espresati's book also contains an introduction with some interesting observations. Many critics have written on Dulcinea, three main directions emerging among their interpretations: (1) that which admits the inaccessible grandeur of Dulcinea as the idealistic exaltation of Platonic love; (2) that which notes that the hyperbolization of the perfections of this figure cause them, automatically, to take on a comic nuance inherent to any exaggeration; and (3) that which attributes a satirical purpose to Cervantes, saying he was alluding to a definite historical person when he contrasted Aldonza and Dulcinea. Conjectures as to the identity of this historical person have ranged from the Virgin Mary to Lope's mistress Micaela de Luján. On the other hand, barely anyone devotes any attention to the "real" person Aldonza Lorenzo, of whom there are three different images in Don Quixote. That in Chapter I is a realistic sketch, the only one which reflects the truth. That in Chapter XXV is idealized by Don Quixote. The third is a caricature by Paniaguado in an epitaph sonnet.

107 Evans, Peter W. "Character and Context in El castigo sin venganza." MLR, 74 (April 1979), 321-34.

Among the characters discussed by Evans are Aurora, Casandra, and Cintia. The questions posed by Lope in this play concern the ways women see themselves in society. Like Tirso and Calderón, Lope strove hard to avoid concentrating excessively on female exploitation, attempting instead to depict the acquiescence of both men and women in debilitating systems of value. All three women in the play are both despised and worshipped; consequently, they are regarded as deviants or misfits. Aurora belongs to the Duke; lives in his shadow; unquestioningly accepts his way of life; welcomes self-effacement to the point of extinction, and would never think of rebelling against a system that steals her uniqueness by compressing her into a masculine effigy of her forbidden self. Casandra is part victim but also part predator. She does not oppose the system itself but complains that she is denied an opportunity to play her proper part in it. In Casandra Lope gives us a vision of a woman seduced by the promise of power, the lure of security, and the esteem that accrues with the transformation of a beautiful body into a useless object of veneration. Cintia's attitude in her confrontation with the Duke is one of the flickering occasions in the play when human nature tries to assert its dignity in the face of almost intolerable pressure from authority. In her refusal to conform, Cintia gives us a glimpse of a nobler world.

108 Feal Deibe, Carlos. "El burlador de Tirso y la mujer." Symposium, 29 (Winter 1975), 300-13.

Don Juan is a diabolical figure in this play, and woman is an amplified projection of the figure of Eve, who can cause man to lose his soul. Tisbea and Isabela are Woman; their sexuality is not a framework in which the personality can express itself, but something which robs their individuality or animalizes them. Ana is linked with women of easy morals, and Aminta is characterized as belonging to a sex essentially perfidious. The burla is thus the just punishment of woman.

109 Fernández Juncos, Manuel. "Las mujeres de Tirso." Nuestro Tiempo, Madrid, 4 (1916), 16-21.

This study takes the form of a dialogue between Tirso and Lope. Tirso's female characters give the impression of falsity, and although there are a few among them who are models of decorum and constancy, the majority represent the most depraved of the species, if indeed such women do exist. In contrast, Lope has not a single unworthy woman.

This difference can be explained by the fact that Lope was personally acquainted with many fine women whom he could use as models, whereas Tirso took his from among his penitents. Tirso's women do, then, have a basis, but these women were, in reality, not so bad as they painted themselves in the confessional.

110 Fernández Suárez, Alvaro. "Sentido y heroísmo del mito de Dulcinea." CA, 6 (November-December 1947), 40-61.
Dulcinea does not come to life with enough power to immediately annihilate Aldonza Lorenzo. Her myth gains strength gradually, affirming itself at the expense of Aldonza, who gave it its pretext and support, and who is finally extinguished. The myth of Dulcinea is perfected and consolidated when Sancho enchants her, since she is then no longer merely an ethereal, insubstantial figure, but a being with external reality.

111 Ferrara de Orduna, Lilia. "Algunas observaciones sobre La Lozana andaluza." Archivum, 23 (1973), 105-15.
Delicado's protagonist appears under three different names, which mark the successive stages in her personality without implying any radical change. All the other characters make Lozana's fundamental traits more salient. She is, among other things, a symbol of Rome and of the sinful city's perdition.

112 Fishlock, A. D. H. "Lope de Vega's La hermosa Ester and Pinto Delgado's 'Poema de la reyna Ester': A Comparative Study." BHS, 32 (April 1955), 81-97.
Fishlock makes a few comments on the figure of Esther. In devotional writing of the period she appears as symbol of the Virgin Mary rather than as interesting for her own sake. Pinto's poem contains none of this traditional Catholic symbolism. Only on stage, however, does Esther come to life as a person, first and chiefly in Lope's La hermosa Ester and later, to a lesser extent, in Dr. Felipe Godínez' Amán y Mardocheo.

113 Fitzmaurice Kelly, Julia. "Women in Sixteenth-Century Spain." Revue Hispanique, 70 (1927), 557-632.
The opinion of woman held by theologians and moralists became a determining factor in her status, since the Church was in effect the State. The monkish idea of woman was accepted by the world at large more generally than is realized. Woman was considered much inferior to man, morally and civilly. For example, Juan Huarte de Sant Juan thinks a woman's brain is not structurally formed to admit of

wisdom or intelligence; her salvation lies, therefore, in subjection and seclusion. The most generous-minded and idealistic authority in the sixteenth century is Luis Vives. From him and from Antonio de Guevara we learn most about a woman's life and training in that period.

When discussing marriage, the moralists characteristically define the wife's duties, while the man is told what qualities to seek in a wife but not those which define his own obligations. The writers are unanimous in the matter of unquestioning obedience on the wife's part. They also agree that physical beauty is a source of danger in matrimony and that love and chastity are the two essential virtues of a wife. The outward observance of a wife's religious duties is subservient to the attention she owes her husband and home. With respect to motherhood, Vives and Luis de León think that if a woman is denied children she should rejoice, since they are a burden and anxiety, and if she does have children, she must not spoil them. Even greater virtue is expected of widows than of wives; the widow should turn her thoughts wholly to heaven.

114 Foa, Sandra M. "Humor and Suicide in Zayas and Cervantes." *ACer*, 16 (1977), 71-83.

Although Zayas's *El castigo de la miseria* was influenced by Cervantes's *El casamiento engañoso*, there are fundamental differences between the two. In Zayas's reduction of the Cervantine characters to one-dimensional caricatures, the original female protagonist, young and beautiful as well as sly, becomes a grotesque figure, an incarnation of deceit, for she feigns not only her wealth but also her youth and good looks. Doña Isidora's function is both to deceive don Marcos and to punish him for his miserliness. Zayas's intention, as Serrano Poncela states (*see* entry 303), is to vindicate feminine astuteness by opposing it to masculine scheming and exploitation. Although Zayas tends to exalt her female protagonists as virginal, saintly, and pure (victims of treachery), she does stress also their intellectual capabilities. In at least one other story she explicitly praises female shrewdness and cunning.

115 _____. "María de Zayas: Visión conflictiva y renuncia del mundo." *CHA*, no. 331 (January 1978), pp. 128-35.

The harmonious vision of love and marriage which characterized so many feminist writings of the sixteenth century is replaced in the seventeenth by a vision of conflict, deceit, and violence. Zayas differs from others in that she presents man and not woman as the chief offender in the war of the sexes. Her female protagonists continually reject marriage either before or after the fact, and enter the convent, a choice clearly favored by the author. Their decision is backed by a long tradition of renunciation of the world. Whereas other writers create characters who are motivated by the resolution to flee temptation and vice, in Zayas's works the women are disillusioned with the treacheries of men.

116 Forcione, Alban K. Cervantes, Aristotle and the Persiles. Princeton, N. J.: Princeton University Press, 1970. See pp. 306-19.

The pages cited above deal with La gitanilla. Preciosa's function as a symbol of poetry is blended with her function as an embodiment of moral perfection. She represents a significant modification of the traditional figure of poetry in that she includes "dark" elements. Preciosa is also an example of Cervantes's heroines who represent the city, their suffering being a symbol of some momentary disorder which afflicts the world of the city and which disappears following their restoration to their proper place in society. Cervantes's often expressed desire to redeem the temptress, such as Carducha in La gitanilla, rather than to severely punish her, reveals the harmonious vision that informs his creation of the novella.

117 Frenk, Margit. "El personaje singular: Un aspecto del teatro del Siglo de Oro." NRFH, 26, no. 2 (1977), 480-98.

There are several cases in the Spanish theater where female figures are characterized through contrastive pairs in which one of the pair may present strange traits. Examples of such pairs are Jacinta and Lucrecia of Alarcón's La verdad sospechosa and Finea and Nise of Lope's La dama boba. Serafina of Tirso's El vergonzoso en palacio has a singular psychological configuration. She is the most noteworthy figure in the play even though she is only tangentially related to the main action.

118 Fucilla, Joseph G. "La dama duende and La viuda valenciana." BCom, 22 (Fall 1970), 29-32.

Both plays are among the few whose leading character is a widow. Leonarda of Lope's La viuda valenciana is a mystery woman, a creature believed to be endowed with supernatural powers. The star of Calderón's La dama duende is a Leonarda shorn of her character, transformed into Angela the pixy.

119 _____. "Finea in Lope's La dama boba in the Light of Modern Psychology." BCom, 7 (Fall 1955), 22-23.

Finea's characterization furnishes a psychological case

history worth considering. Her initial stupidity is not congenital, as evidenced by her subsequent brightness. The motivating explanation of her first state is found in her sister Nise, whose cleverness, refinement, and high degree of culture have made her the center of attention. Finea has reacted by going to the opposite extreme; she is not feebleminded but psychopathic.

120 Garasa, Delfín Leocadio. "Circe en la literatura española del Siglo de Oro." *Boletín de la Academia Argentina de Letras*, 29, nos. 112-13 (April-September 1964), 227-71.

Circe is a common figure to poets, narrative writers, and moralists of the Golden Age. Less complex than the original, as found in Homer, she is above all a witch or sorceress, and her name signifies a dangerous woman capable of causing any man to be lost through her evil arts.

After quoting from various Golden Age writers, Garasa deals in detail with two works: Lope's *La Circe* and Calderón's *El mayor encanto amor*. Lope probably wanted to restore to the myth of Circe its profound reality, but in the last analysis he transforms her from her primitive and ferocious condition of *maga* into an afflicted and intensely passionate woman. Calderón was the first to dramatize the myth of Circe in Spain. Not surprisingly for a Baroque writer, fond of transformations, ever-changing forms, and the play between the apparent and the real, Calderón exploits Circe's character as enchantress. In his *auto sacramental* *Los encantos de la Culpa*, Circe is identified with Culpa.

121 García, William B. "Algo más sobre el episodio del Cautivo." *AC*, 12 (1973), 187-90.

The motives which inspired Zoraida in her relationship with the Captive were genuinely religious. Her conversion is essential to the development of the episode, since it is her faith which gives her confidence for her dangerous adventure. Zoraida's response to the spiritual apparition of the dead Christian slave woman gives us an idea of her personality. She is perhaps the only person in the novel besides Don Quixote who receives messages from the other world. Her earlier decision is confirmed by this event, which causes her to feel completely justified in abandoning not only her country but also the father whom she loves so much, entrusting herself to a stranger and to a future which would be very uncertain if not seen with the eyes of faith. Cervantes makes it clear that it was the Virgin Mary who sent the slave woman on her supernatural mission, in order that Zoraida might not forget the teachings she had received and her obligation to confirm them in Baptism.

122 García Nieto, José. "Una 'mujer' en el teatro de Tirso." Consigna, no. 99 (April 1949), pp. 12-14.
Tirso's predilection for carefully elaborated feminine types is evident from the numerous plays which bear the name of the feminine protagonist. Among all his women, so varied and so fascinating, Violante of La villana de Vallecas holds an outstanding place.

123 Gerchunoff, Alberto. "Dulcinea del Toboso." RHM, 23, nos. 3-4 (1957), 349-50.
This is an excerpt from the author's La jofaina maravillosa.

124 _____. La jofaina maravillosa: Agenda cervantina. Third Edition. Buenos Aires: M. Gleizer, 1927.
Gerchunoff's book contains several sections on female figures in Cervantes's works. Preciosa, one of his most living and memorable characters, represents the mysterious woman of Spain's prohibited races. In her, Cervantes sums up the grace, litheness, and voice characteristic of the Mooress and, at the same time, of a thousand heroines of fantasy. Luscinda is typical of Cervantes's women, with her common sense, ingenuity, sweetness and tenderness, mixture of decorum and irresistible appeal, and, above all, fidelity. Zoraida is the synthesis of all those Moorish women created by the poets and revived by the memories of those returning from captivity. By freeing a Christian captive and becoming Christian herself, she realizes the double ideal of the Spaniard of that time. Galatea, unlike Marcela, is an alabaster statue, a goddess, more than a living being. She is a literary woman who knows all will turn out well in the end. Dulcinea is the key to the Quixote. In her, the hero shows us the eternal presence of woman, apart from whom nothing great or lofty has been done or thought.

125 Gijón Zapata, Esmeralda. "Concepto del honor y la mujer en Tirso de Molina." Estudios, 5, nos. 13-15 (1949), 479-655.
Apart from Cervantes, no Golden Age writer understood the feminine soul so well as Tirso. Lope's respect for women was more fictitious and external, at least until his last works. Some explain Tirso's comprehension as the result of his activities as a confessor, but Gijón thinks it was due to his love, which gave him a special way of seeing. Tirso's works manifest filoginia, not feminismo. A superficial reading might point out misogynistic traits in many of his characters, but this apparently negative attitude toward women is refuted many times over by such

facts as the following: (1) Tirso presents the honor problem from the feminine rather than the masculine point of view; (2) he advocates respect for all women, not just the virtuous; (3) he considers the pressure of the passions on woman as well as man; (4) he distinguishes between the woman who errs through passion or weakness, and who is often the victim of deception, and the one who perseveres in sin through ambition or caprice; (5) he rejects the "testing" of women; and (6) he uses an authentic language to express a woman's sorrow and other emotions.

126 _____. El humor en Tirso de Molina. Madrid: Gráficas H. de la Guardia Civil, 1959. See especially Chs. 4 and 6.

In these sections Gijón Zapata treats Tirso's graciosas and antitenorios. Tirso was a unique painter of feminine portraits in the theater, as Céspedes y Meneses was in the novela cortesana. Perhaps Tirso's most successful female figures are his graciosas, a group which includes criadas, pastoras, serranas, and villanas. Though they are less numerous than the graciosos, perhaps because of the abundance of comic female protagonists, there are more than fifty graciosas in Tirso's plays. His liking for them is evident through the beauty he gives them and his custom of opposing them to damas linajudas, a rivalry in which the graciosas always emerge triumphant. Negative qualities found in some are doubtful loyalty to one's mistress, and impulsive, unreflecting behavior mixed with considerable liviandad. Positive qualities include ingeniousness and wit; loyalty, often accompanied by a delicate maternal solicitude; strength, and especially courage. Preeminent among all the graciosas is Antona García, in whom the humorous villana and the popular hero are fused. She is a symbol of feminine integrity in the same way as María de Molina.

The antitenorio, an original interpretation of the tenorio's victim, exemplifies woman's conquest of sorrow and passion through wit. Her role is usually to confront and conquer the trickster, after having first driven him to desperation through ridicule. This type par excellence is found in Don Gil de las calzas verdes, in which the heroine is, as it were, pure ingenio but with a certain indispensable amount of passion.

127 Gillet, Joseph E. "Lucrecia-necia." HR, 15 (January 1947), 120-36.

Lucretia, once the ideal embodiment of tragic purity, became an example of foolish and lewd behavior for many Golden Age writers--though not for all and not consistently--in great part because of the simplification of a passage on suicide in St. Augustine's City of God. In the Baroque period Lucretia suffered, as did Dido and other long-revered figures, from the debunking process. It was an age losing faith in itself. Its process of self-destruction began by denying that there was any virtue left in women, and ended by affirming there never had been, that no woman was ever forced, and that Lucretia must have been both a wanton and a hypocrite. In addition, the greater frequency with which *Lucrecia* is rhymed with *necia* in the Baroque reflects the new emphasis on *discreción*; Lucretia is regarded as a fool for having committed suicide.

128 Glaser, Edward. "Calderón de la Barca's *La sibila del Oriente y gran reina de Saba*." *RF*, 72 (1960), 381-403.

Calderón's dramatic portrayal of Sheba, the Old Testament queen whom legend had fused with the Babylonian sibyl, emphasizes the seer at the expense of the ruler and the woman. As queen, and as a woman of exceptional intellectual powers in which she takes deep pride, Sheba is moved to undertake the arduous journey to Jerusalem not by a thirst for wisdom but by the challenge of a famed competitor. Nevertheless, this self-possessed queen, patterned after the haughty women who abound in Calderón's theater, wields scarcely any influence over the action which is dominated by the sibyl; one who embodies the traditional image of the ancient soothsayers. Through her, God leads Solomon to spiritual maturity.

129 _____. "Lope de Vega's *La hermosa Ester*." *Sefarad*, 20 (1960), 110-35.

Lope radically changes the features of the Biblical figure of Esther. Whereas the latter is at best an indifferent adherent of Judaism, who raises no objection to changing her religion or marrying a Gentile, in the play she is transformed into a model servant of the Eternal, self-effacing and pious. Lope has her captivate the king with her beauty of soul, as much as with her physical charms. Though the latter are mentioned, it is her meekness which stands out most vividly. Besides being a Biblical heroine, Esther is also in this play a figure of the Virgin Mary.

130 _____. "*La mejor espigadera* de Tirso de Molina." *Les Lettres Romanes*, 14 (1960), 199-218.

The play contrasts *pietas* and *impietas*, both Noemi and Ruth being examples of the former. Noemi manifests this virtue by her solicitude for the poor and needy; Ruth, by her total devotion to God and to the aged and poor Noemi. Ruth is obedient to divine inspiration at all times, her interest in Mahalon being no exception to this rule. The frequently recalled fact that the former princess voluntarily becomes a humble gleaner is offered as a particularly striking illustration of her charity. For a seventeenth-century audience, sweetness and obedience, far from being minor virtues, would denote unusual perfection and would add substantially to the attractiveness of the portrayal of Ruth's holiness.

131 _____. "Santa Isabel, Reina de Portugal, de Francisco de Rojas Zorrilla." Estudios hispano-portugueses: Relaciones literarias del Siglo de Oro. Madrid: Castalia, 1957, pp. 179-220.

Golden Age writers are, in general, more interested in the superhuman actions of Isabel than in her virtues. This emphasis tends to overshadow her human aspect. Rojas Zorrilla, however, centers his interest on the woman, whom he presents at a moment of grave crisis. She is not, as Américo Castro suggests, simply a stubborn woman who disdains the demands of a weak husband, but a serene, dignified, and profoundly religious woman, for whom Christ's precepts prevail over anyone else's. Yet when her husband comes to doubt her fidelity, she suffers greatly and exhausts every fitting human means to save her marriage. Even with her attributes of sanctity, she is not a female Job. Her preoccupation over her marriage gives her a deeply feminine charm which the hagiographical writings do not bring out.

132 _____. "Tirso de Molina's La mujer que manda en casa." Annali Istituto Universitario Orientale, Napoli, Sezione Romanza, 2 (1960), 25-42.

Contrary to many assertions, Jezebel does not undergo an inner development in this play but invariably typifies the homo carnalis. Since Tirso follows the tradition, according to which Jezebel is the embodiment of lust, the assumption that under the guise of a Biblical tale he is attacking the domineering Margaret of Austria seems farfetched.

In the first two acts, Rachel is a loyal but intensely jealous wife. Under the impact of tragedy, she becomes, in the third act, the champion of traditional Jewry, taking her husband's place as the principal antagonist of Queen Jezebel.

133 Goggio, Emilio. "The Dual Role of Dulcinea in Cervantes' Don Quijote de la Mancha." Modern Language Quarterly, 13 (September 1952), 285-91.

After summarizing several earlier interpretations of Dulcinea, Goggio states that there are two different Dulcineas, or rather, that she has two roles. One is the destruction of the vogue of the romances of chivalry; the other, the revival of the practice of the lofty ideals which formed the real essence of the old romances. In the first case, Dulcinea is Aldonza Lorenzo; a woman of flesh and blood, uninspiring and unattractive, an instrument of parody and satire. In the second case, Dulcinea is a symbol of beauty, goodness, and grace; endowed with all the finest physical and spiritual qualities which poets of all ages applied to the beloved. Cervantes combines these with moral virtues which the later Provençal poets and Petrarch attributed to their ladies and to the Virgin Mary, making Dulcinea the supreme example of the courtly lady. One point of view emerges from the other; both are the projection of Don Quixote's imagination.

134 Gómez de la Serna, Ramón. "Quevedo y las mujeres." Clavileño, 1, no. 3 (1950), 63-68.
The author does not agree with those who label Quevedo an enemy of women. His twenty-odd sonnets against women cannot stand up against his more than two hundred love poems. Quevedo's antifeminist satire was meant to evoke laughter from his reading public, but it does not mean he himself was a misogynist.

135 Goyanes, Dr. J. Tipología de El Quijote: Ensayo sobre la estructura psicosomática de los personajes de la novela. Madrid: S. Aguirre, 1932.
The study includes sections on Dulcinea and Maritornes. Dulcinea is a very clear symbol of love in the Augustinian sense. Just as for Augustine, love descends from on high to elevate what is lowly to itself, so Don Quixote descends from the sublime symbol of his love to the lowliness of the real nature of his lady, in order to elevate and idealize it.
Maritornes is a tipo cretino. This is manifested by her particular kind of bodily deformity, and by her temperament, which marks her as libidinous and malicious, with a quickness for evildoing and deceit, yet with a sentimental compassion for men.

136 Goyri de Menéndez Pidal, María. "La Celia de Lope de Vega." NRFH, 4, no. 4 (1950), 347-90.
In his literary works, Lope has left us such detailed portraits of the women he loved that they are easily distinguishable one from the other. For example, Elena Osorio can be identified by her green, somewhat bold eyes, black brows and lashes, smiling mouth, clear complexion, and long, slim hands. This portrait, which was for many years the ideal of feminine beauty, is also used by Lope for Eve and the Virgin Mary. Marta de Nevares has emerald eyes, chaster than Elena's, blonde hair, and intellectual gifts greater

than those of Lope's other loves. Micaela de Luján has blue eyes, curly hair, a rose and white complexion, an angelical voice, and a snowy bosom. The fictitious names Celia and Lucinda probably both refer to Micaela.

137 Grant, Helen F. "The World Upside-Down." Studies in Spanish Literature of the Golden Age Presented to Edward M. Wilson. Edited by R. O. Jones. London: Tamesis Bks., Ltd., 1973, pp. 103-35.

The topos of the world upside-down, that is, one in which the divine order is upset, includes the reversal of the roles of men and women. The most popular image for representing such inversion, that of the man holding the distaff, and the woman, the sword, or beating metal on the forge, has its origin in the legend of Hercules and Omphale. Calderón's Fieras afemina amor and Gracián's El criticón make use of this tradition. Calerón is sympathetic to the female, who revenges herself for Hercules's brutish behavior by turning him into an effete creature. Even Gracián, no admirer of women, finds man's bestiality more to blame for unhinging the world than the faults of womankind.

On the whole, the reversal of sex roles is condemned in Spanish literature, nor are the Amazons looked on with favor. The best thing that happens to them is that they fall in love with the male enemy, as in Antonio de Solís's Las amazonas.

138 Guillén, Diego Gracia. "Chirino en El retablo de las maravillas." PSA, 92, nos. 274-76 (January-March 1979), 9-27.

La Chirinos of Cervantes's entremés is a conversa and the designer of the farce.

139 Güntert, Georges. "La Gitanilla y la poética de Cervantes." BRAE, 52 (January-April 1972), 107-34.

Cervantes causes the two planes of the material and the spiritual to converge in the figure of Preciosa through the image of the jewel, simultaneously valuable and virtuous. Through the same image Preciosa is made to symbolize poetry, a jewel exiled in a world beautified by its presence.

140 Gutiérrez, María del Carmen. "As personages femininas na dramática de Tirso de Molina." Universitárias, Lisbon. Fourth series, no. 23 (January 1949), 21-26.

Tirso's feminine characters are as varied as the subject matter of his plays, for his feminine psychology embraces every type. Gutiérrez discusses the heroines of La mejor espigadera, La prudencia en la mujer, Marta la piadosa, and El amor y el amistad. In the portrayal of certain feminine types, such as those found in the comedias villanescas and the plays of intrigue, Tirso puts too much emphasis on the deceits and miseries of youth. He also overuses the masculine disguise.

141 Gutiérrez, Violeta. "La Celestina en las comedias de Lope de Vega." ExTL, 4, no. 2 (1975-76), 161-68.

Gutiérrez concentrates mainly on El Caballero de Olmedo, although she briefly mentions El galán escarmentado, El galán Castrucho, and Por la puente de Juana. Celestina's influence is clearly seen in the character of Fabia. Both women are witches, have the ability to repair lost virginity, and manifest astuteness in leading the young women to sin. Inés differs from Melibea in her reaction to the procuress. Whereas Melibea at first objects violently to Celestina's intervention, Inés accepts Fabia as intermediary from the beginning. In both works we see social criticism of the form of life to which women of the period were condemned in order to preserve their virtue.

142 Hanrahan, Thomas. La mujer en la novela picaresca de Mateo Alemán. Madrid: José Porrúa Turanzas, 1964.

Woman plays an important role in Guzmán de Alfarache, even though she does not occupy center stage. The depiction of the more than twenty-five female characters in the novel, taken from all the social classes, is virtually always a deformation. The consistently negative valuation of women, more pessimistic than is called for by the picaresque genre itself, is conscious and preconceived on the author's part. The good woman is almost nonexistent for Alemán, since woman is not only, by nature, less endowed than man to live a virtuous life, and spontaneously deceitful (Part I); but the root of sin, possessing a will ordained to sin (Part II). The woman is always culpable for the troubles of man, taking advantage of his erotic blindness whenever possible. After relegating woman to an inferior position, Alemán then condemns her for acting in the only way open for the underdog to get what she wants. Alemán's attitude toward women is due in great part to the split in his psyche, to his struggles with concupiscence, which he sees as evil and identifies with its object, woman.

143 _____. La mujer en la novela picaresca española. Madrid: José Porrúa Turanzas, 1967.

The role and concept of woman in the most representative picaresque works correlates with the ascetic-didactic purpose of the genre. Since the pícaro is an example of how not to live, the women who pass through his life will not be virtuous. Moreover, the strong antifeminist tradition of ascetic literature, with its preconceived notions of the nature of woman, made it difficult for her to be treated favorably in such a genre.

The view of woman in the picaresque is conditioned by the atmosphere of the Counter Reformation and differs from the misogyny of medieval writers or Italian novelists. All authors of picaresque works agree in presenting woman as an object of concupiscence, an evil to be avoided, attractive but dangerous, and extremely deceitful. Because of her astuteness she is the major obstacle in man's way to perfection. The lesson is the same as that of the desert Fathers: man is better off alone. It can be said that if an author does not present woman in this way, he has not written a picaresque novel.

On this basis Hanrahan compares and contrasts the way women are depicted in a number of works which have at one time or another been labeled picaresque. One chapter discusses Cervantes, Alemán, and Quevedo; another, the so-called _pícaras_ Justina, Elena, and Teresa and Rufina, heroines created by Francisco López de Ubeda, Salas Barbadillo, and Castillo Solórzano, respectively; a third, Vicente Espinel, Jerónimo Alcalá Yáñez, and Juan Martí; and yet another; the exiles Antonio Enríquez Gómez, Juan de Luna, and Carlos García.

144 Hart, Thomas R., and Steven Rendall. "Rhetoric and Persuasion in Marcela's Address to the Shepherds." _HR_, 46 (Summer 1978), 287-98.

Although Marcela's speech is very reasonable, the _ethos_ she projects tends to confirm the charge that she is cruel and insensitive, a proud creature incapable of sympathy with others. The shepherds may well see her as an embodiment of the _mujer esquiva_, an important type in the _comedia_ at the time the _Quixote_ first appeared. In this case her disdain is an attitude not destined to last, and her cruelty to Grisóstomo is all the more reprehensible since it implies that her reasons for rejecting him are based on a mistaken notion of her own ability to escape the tyranny of love. Marcela rejects not only Grisóstomo's suit but the very institution of marriage, which means rejecting society itself in the context of the times. Her excessive concern with her selfhood ends in self-love, as proved by the fact that she uses her suitor's grave as a tribunal from which to plead her own cause. Cervantes did not intend, as Mary Mackey suggests (_see_ entry 201), that Marcela serve as a standard by which to judge Don Quixote. Both characters reflect the tendency to confuse what is possible in literature with what is possible in life.

145 Haverbeck Ojeda, Erwin. "La astucia femenina en el teatro clásico español." Stylo, 5, no. 8 (1969), 25-81.

The study is based primarily on four of Tirso's plays: El vergonzoso en palacio, Marta la piadosa, Don Gil de las calzas verdes, and El amor médico, and secondarily on about sixteen other comedias. The predominant theme in these plays is love which arises between equals, a love which once awakened must be legalized and sanctified through marriage. The female characters assume the initiative and are responsible for overcoming the diverse obstacles to the achievement of the proper end. To do so they consciously employ capacities considered essentially feminine. Astuteness is the basic one, which orients everything the woman does and underlies such traits as her great facility in speech, rapid inventiveness in solving problems, and ability to hide her true feelings. These women are also unmarried, of high social class, beautiful in a stereotyped fashion, personally winsome, virtuous, and deeply impressed by a galán's heroism as well as his handsome appearance. If any of them manifest some other preoccupation than love, such as a desire for liberty, learning, or a career, it is always transitory and in the end subordinated to love.

An evident community of feeling is created between the feminine protagonist and the spectators. All the male characters appear as credulous and easy to deceive; the woman is almost always in control of the complex situations she creates. One explanation for the happy ending is that since the Renaissance, there appears in literature the theme of a woman's right to freely choose her husband. Another is that love has a social dimension, and that she who stimulates a man's eroticism must transform his desire into a social and religious impulse.

146 _____. "La 'dama boba' en el teatro clásico español." Stylo, 3, no. 8 (1966), 21-41.

Closely related to Dorotea of the Quixote are a series of female characters in the Spanish Golden Age theater. Like her, they are beautiful, desenvueltas, discreet, with a gift for words, often obliged to wear men's clothing and to fight in order to win their objective, which is usually to marry a certain gentleman. They achieve their aim principally through their astuteness, which in several cases consists in pretending to be boba. Two examples are the heroines of Lope de Vega's La dama boba and La boba para los otros y discreta para sí.

147 Hernández de Mendoza, Cecilia. Para una biografía de Dulcinea del Toboso. Bogotá: Antena, 1948. Also in RdA, 13 (1948), 385-402.

Dulcinea contains in herself the feminine types of Aldonza Lorenzo and the village lass. Book I, Chapter 25 gives us a portrait of Aldonza through which we understand how Alonso de Quijada could love in her the gracia, life, and nature which he never glimpsed in the mediocre leisure of his retirement. By changing her name, he changes her personality. Book I, Chapter 13 provides a description of Dulcinea in which we glimpse the ideal of feminine beauty in the Golden Age, while Book II, Chapter 32 allows us to glimpse the ideal of feminine personality. As a personal creation of Don Quixote, Dulcinea belongs to him intimately. She is the most noble part of his yo; the symbol of the sublime aspect of his personality. Her biography is nothing other than the ideal biography of Don Quixote. Cervantes identifies the integral man in two personalities; the woman, in only one, changed by enchantments. In so doing he speaks clearly of the psychological difference between man and woman. Man can be part prose and part ideal at the same time, whereas woman is sometimes integrally prose and other times integrally ensueño.

148 Hernández Ortiz, José A. La génesis artística de la Lozana andaluza: El realismo literario de Francisco Delicado. Madrid: Aguilera, 1974.

The study includes a section on Lozana as central figure of the novel and one on its feminism. Lozana is like a representation of Mother Nature, concretely, Andalusian nature. She is motivated principally by her natural biological instincts. The first individualized heroine of the lower class in a degraded society, she shares archetypal characteristics of the hero: will, vigor, impetuosity, pujanza, plenitude, an interior, almost automatic discipline of the vital impulses, and the struggle with the society which she must conquer.

The novel is unique in its presentation of the feminine world in an ambience of vice and prostitution. The work revolves, in general, around the feminine characters, giving a vivid and direct document of their lives. The author achieves a realistic picture of woman by avoiding extremes and explaining character through the struggle with and adaptation to the environment.

149 Herrero, Javier. "Arcadia's Inferno: Cervantes' Attack on Pastoral." BHS, 55 (October 1978), 289-99.

In the Marcela-Grisóstomo episode of the Quixote, Cervantes attacks the knightly and pastoral concept of love which made adoration of woman the center of man's moral existence. The god of love in chivalry and pastoral is really the devil, who exhibits his cruelty by inflicting the poison of love upon his victims through the beauty of women. Thus, the shepherdess and Diana-like goddess Marcela is an instrument of the demon of love.

The great mistake of the worshippers of woman was to expect perfection in the object of love. True lovers are those who help each other overcome their imperfections and develop their potential through the mutual support found in marriage. It is no accident that the hardhearted women who cannot surrender to the imperfection of a human embrace, Marcela and Leandra, both lack mothers; they have no experience of the limitations of human love.

Dulcinea can be found only after death, and if we mistakenly search for her in this life, we shall find Diana-Hecate, the mythical goddess-sorceress, who transforms men into beasts.

150 Herrero-García, Miguel. Estimaciones literarias del siglo XVII. Madrid: Editorial Voluntad, 1930. See pp. 9-60.

The author discusses the influence of the Celestina on various works by seventeenth-century Spanish writers. Aspects of the character Celestina reflected in later figures are her expertise in the arts of love, witchcraft, religious hypocrisy, lying and trickery, and addiction to wine. There is no doubt that in the thought of these writers Celestina was projected whole and entire, but this thought is represented in their characters fragmentarily.

151 Hershberg, David. "Porcia in Golden Age Literature: Echoes of a Classical Theme." Neophil, 54 (January 1970), 22-27.

Although she is never the central figure of a comedia, Portia attracted the attention of many Golden Age writers of prose and poetry, as cited by Hershberg. Those few who fault her, find her most reprehensible for her indirect participation in the assassination of Caesar, which constituted a rebellion against established authority. More numerous, however, are those who praise her for her dedicated love and self-sacrifice.

152 Hesse, Everett W. "El conflicto entre madre e hijos en Los melindres de Belisa de Lope." Hispania, 54 (December 1971), 836-43.

Lope draws Lisarda as a restless widow who seeks a husband, though she denies this. Incapable of confronting reality, she cannot believe her children have grown up and insists on imposing her own will, treating them as if they were infants. She does not realize that by spoiling them in their early years she has ruined their lives. She is the epitome of incomprehension and egotism.

The portrait of Belisa, the daughter, is more complex and attractive. Spoiled and capricious, intelligent and astute, she is the only person who understands the cause of her melindres, and she learns something in the course of events.

153 _____. "Estructura e interpretación de una comedia de Calderón: Eco y Narciso." Filología, 7 (1961), 61-76.
The thematic profundity of this play resides in the powerful dominion of the mother over an innocent son, and in the tragic consequences of her actions which are due to her erroneous philosophy. The principal theme of unreciprocated love depends on the repressive influence of the mother, motivated, according to Hesse, by purely egotistic reasons (although he later admits a combination of egotistic and altruistic motives).

154 _____. "Lope's La discreta enamorada and the Generation Gap." Hispano, no. 44 (January 1972), pp. 1-12.
The split between mother and daughter in this play stems largely from a clash over the latter's behavior in seeking a husband. On the other hand, the daughter detects hypocrisy in her widowed mother's actions, and the older woman is made to look foolish when she thinks a younger man has a romantic interest in her.

155 _____. "The 'Terrible Mother' Image in Calderón's Eco y Narciso." RomN, 1 (Spring 1960), 133-36.
The real import of the play for the modern reader is the overriding power of the "terrible mother" on an innocent son and the tragic consequences of her action and misapprehension. Hesse speaks of Liríope's inner bestiality and fierce nature, and labels her a proud mother guided by self-interest and by a sense of guilt and dishonor.

156 Heugas, Pierre. La Célestine et sa descendance directe. Bordeaux: Institut d'Études Ibériques et Ibéro-Americaines de l'Université de Bordeaux, 1973. See especially pp. 355-408, 457-539.
The first of the above sections discusses the heroines of the Celestina and its imitations; the second, underworld characters in the same works, including prostitutes of various categories and the procuress type. The fundamental continuity among the works is borne out in their central characters. Even those heroines who are less tragic and more bourgeois than the original, and who express their amorous feeling in a new rhetoric, are Melibean heroines because they still correspond to the conception of love and

Heugas

of woman which prevailed in the Middle Ages. Because of their essential frailty as women they succumb to the Celestina type and to illicit love. Areusa and Elicia, two of the original low figures who appear in the imitations, undergo a progressive degradation.

157 _____. "Variation sur un portrait: De Mélibée a Dulcinée." BH, 71 (1969), 5-30.
In both the Celestina and Don Quixote we find criticism of the conception of the lady which had been initiated with the courtly tradition. The Celestina, however, parodies the medieval portrait in a subtler fashion than that in which Cervantes mocks the sixteenth-century dama of the poets. The latter was a modified version of the medieval prototype, which soon became just as stereotyped and monotonous as the original. No one has shown better the collapse of the myth of the dama than Cervantes, through the creation of the mythical Dulcinea. On some occasions he uses playful banter; on others, such as in Part I, Chapter 31, the frankly parodical anti-portrait, comparable to Elicia and Areusa's description of Melibea in Act 9 of the Celestina. The delineation of Maritornes, who belongs to a tradition which includes the serranas of the Arcipreste de Hita and certain figures of Cristóbal de Castillejo, is a rough draft of the anti-portrait of Dulcinea. There is no idealized female in the whole Quixote, and only one evocation of feminine beauty, Dorotea's, which is not later made ambiguous.

158 Holloway, James E., Jr. "Lope's Neoplatonism: La dama boba." BHS, 49 (July 1972), 236-55.
Nise is usually considered to function in contrast to Finea. She highlights the latter's deficiencies and emphasizes her development when both come to strive for the attentions of the same lover. They are indeed opposites from the point of view that both are extremes, and that their respective excesses jeopardize the achievement of a goal which God and society intend for them, the sacrament of marriage. Finea, who is initially sense and appetite, must give up her bestial nature for a spiritually mature state. Nise, who is reason and choice, must give up her pride in her intelligence in order to acquire true wisdom, which lies beyond reason. She proves to be slower than Finea in finding love and developing her potential of entendimiento.

159 Honig, Edwin. "Flickers of Incest on the Face of Honor: The Phantom Lady." Tulane Drama Review, 6 (1962), 69-105.

Also in Calderón and the Seizures of Honor. Cambridge: Harvard University Press, 1972, pp. 110-57.

Seen in conjunction with Calderón's other honor plays, The Phantom Lady presents a woman's rebellion against the autocratic male principles of the code, as she seeks to achieve the liberty to love whom she pleases. Part of Angela's justification is the wish to cast off the impending threat of incest, however unconscious it may be. She works out her assault on constituted authority within the framework of that authority, and because she is a woman-with-a-cause and the ethos she acts in is the social ethos of comedy, she shares her purpose with female accomplices who help to penetrate her isolation.

160 Horst, Robert ter. "The Ruling Temper of Calderón's La dama duende." BCom, 27 (Fall 1975), 68-72.

Manuel, who represents the play's aspiration to order, is the protagonist, while Angela, who describes its path to chaos, is the antagonist. She suffers more from bad government than from chauvinist oppression, since in Calderonian terms one must accept her brother's close supervision of her as natural and just. Angela is a disobedient angel descending, but in the end Manuel tames his splendid shrew.

161 ______. "The True Mind of Marriage: Ironies of the Intellect in Lope's La dama boba." RJ, 27 (1976), 347-63.

In this interested worldly parody of disinterested literary love, woman is a commodity, a basic mechanism of domestic economy. The concerns of the men who seek wives are, in order of importance; money, biological capacity, ability to manage children and home, beauty, and, in a very limited sense, intelligence. Finea's awakening to intelligence means that she recognizes the male mind as absolutely dominant and worships its supremacy. One of the most discouraging aspects of the play is the insinuation that women really need no mind of their own and that their highest intelligence is manifested in the use of marital wiles that feign cleverness (as with Nise) or pretend a stupidity which does not truly represent them (as with Finea).

162 Illanes Adaro, Graciela. "Figuras femeninas del Quijote." Atenea: Revista de Ciencia, Arte y Literatura de la Universidad de Concepción, Chile, no. 268 (October 1947), pp. 156-67.

The author discusses briefly the character or significance of several women of the Quixote. For example, the housekeeper and niece are symbols of abnegation and affection; Dulcinea is woman as ideal, illusion, and hope; Marcela represents beauty, discretion, chastity, and integrity; Madásima is the untouched woman; Leandra symbolizes the unattainable, the elusiveness of reality; and Urganda is the kind of creation needed by Don Quixote to blame for his misfortunes and to invoke in the midst of them. Maritornes is not charitable, but unkind, and Luscinda is all submission, incapable of saying no to her parents.

163 Iventosch, Herman. "Cervantes and Courtly Love: The Grisóstomo-Marcela Episode of Don Quixote." PMLA, 89 (January 1974), 64-76.
In this episode Cervantes gives a simple and prosaic answer to the whole grandiose edifice of Petrarchism and its cruel females. Marcela has humdrum reasons for not loving.

164 _____. "Dulcinea, nombre pastoril." NRFH, 17, nos. 1-2 (1963-64), 60-81.
The chivalresque world is completely absent from the name Dulcinea; a person, moreover, as passive and denaturalized as predecessors like Oriana were active and sensual. Dulcinea is named pastorally at the beginning, and always keeps something of that early configuration. But her name attracts to itself essences of the dulce of Petrarch's dulces enemigas and also of the immemorial dulzura of the Virgin, so vividly represented in Don Quixote's lady, his guide and north star, the only refuge of his hopes.

165 Jarnés, Benjamín. "Altisidora." Mañana, México (29 April, 1944), pp. 76-77.
Altisidora is the mature fruit of Cervantes's writing, his last creation and perhaps the most cherished. In her figure, gracia infiltrates humor and vice versa. She could only emerge from an enkindled intelligence, illumined by the heart, that is, the complete man. Altisidora is the feminine Cervantes. She is also the woman of the twentieth century.

166 _____. "La desenvuelta Altisidora." RdA, 7 (1946), 81-88.
Jarnés gives an imaginative account of Altisidora's inner world. Altisidora is Cervantes himself; she fell in love with Don Quixote with the same tenderness Cervantes did. She knew Don Quixote as the hero of a book in which she dreamed of participating, and since he did not allow her to penetrate his intimacy, she could not let him escape without becoming part of his picturesque life.

167 Jiménez, Julio. "Doña Mariana de Carvajal y Saavedra, mujer

y escritora en la España de los Felipes." ExTL, 6, no. 2 (1978), 205-13.

The women who appear in Carvajal's Navidades de Madrid y noches entretenidas are mostly single or widows. The latter differ from widows presented in the theater in that they have serious responsibilities.

Carvajal's moral criticism, when present, is against women when they fail to live up to what they owe themselves. It is, thus, directed to maintaining woman's position in society.

168 Johnson, Leslie Deutsch. "Three Who Made a Revolution: Cervantes, Galatea and Caliope." Hispano, no. 57 (May 1976), pp. 23-33.

In Cervantes's Galatea, the mythical figure is brought to life with human weaknesses and frailties. Though the description of her is by no means unsympathetic, she is relieved of the burden of living on a pedestal. Like Preciosa of La gitanilla, Galatea represents Poetry, which corresponds closely to Cervantes's ideal of feminine beauty. The rigid figure of Gelasia is the unobtainable, unreal aspect of the myth that Galatea has in many ways abandoned.

169 José Prades, Juana de. Teoría sobre los personajes de la Comedia Nueva, en cinco dramaturgos. Madrid: Consejo Superior de Investigaciones Científicas, 1963.

Among the six character types discussed are the dama and the criada. In the amorous comedias studied, the creations of five contemporaries and disciples of Lope de Vega, the dama is always beautiful; of aristocratic background; dedicated exclusively to the fulfillment of her love for the galán, and, in order to achieve this, capable of using audacity and dissimulation.

The criada is the devoted companion of the dama, who sometimes brings about the latter's amorous initiatives; covers up her love affairs; acts as astute counselor and able mediator, and is inclined toward the gracioso with whom she reproduces on a parodic level the love of dama and galán, and whose greed and self-interest she matches. Exceptions to this unwritten formula, which does allow for variation, only prove the rule.

170 Juliá Martí, Eduardo. Las mujeres valencianas en las comedias de Lope de Vega. Madrid: Librería Tormes, 1941.

There is not, in the approximately eight plays of Lope which embody a Valencian influence, any study of the psychology of Valencian women. Instead, Lope offers in these female protagonists, an exposition of characters who are basically the products of his intimate life, while the secondary female characters are completely influenced by Italian works.

171 Kahiluoto Rudat, Eva M. "Ilusión y desengaño: El feminismo barroco de María de Zayas y Sotomayor." Letras femeninas, 1, no. 1 (1975), 27-43.

The purpose of Zayas's novelas is to illustrate the situation of woman in society, with the double aim of defense and warning. In the second part of her collection the stories are meant to show that men are chiefly culpable for all the sufferings of women, especially those of innocent women. The feminist theme is already implicit in the first part, but at that time Zayas was apparently still confident that women's intelligence could effect improvement in their social situation. This attitude changes visibly in the second part, in which the only solution seen as available to women is the convent.

Some of the points in Zayas's feminist theory are that women are spiritually equal to men, since they have the same soul, which is neither masculine nor feminine; that the lack of learned women is due only to the lack of opportunity to develop their intellectual capacity; that men have deprived women of access to arms and letters out of fear and envy; that men have made women weaker than nature has; and that there is a need for women writers, since all literary works of the time are offensive to women, being written by men and from the male point of view. Her affirmations regarding the intelligence of woman seem a direct answer to authors like Gracián, who says in his Agudeza y arte de ingenio that the capacity of the most intelligent woman does not surpass that of any fourteen-year-old male.

172 Kennedy, Ruth Lee. The Dramatic Art of Moreto. Smith College Studies in Modern Languages, 13, nos. 1-4. Northampton, Mass.: n.p., 1932. See especially pp. 86-94.

Indispensable terms for describing Moreto's heroines are recato, decoro, respeto, and discreción, just as brío is for those of Lope. Moreto's women exhibit decorum in every relationship of life; as sweetheart or wife, daughter or sister, even as feminine rival. Their decorum has its roots in an innate sense of dignity and self-respect. Moreto avoids such situations as the rivalry of mother and daughter, the triangle involving an unfaithful wife, the heroine in search of a faithless lover, and the masculine disguise. His heroines, and heroes, mirror the immense respect Moreto felt for womanhood.

173 ______. "La prudencia en la mujer and the Ambient (sic) that Brought It Forth." PMLA, 63 (1948), 1131-90.
Kennedy agrees with Blanca de los Ríos that Tirso has glorified María de Molina in her triple majesty: as heroic queen, magnanimous toward her enemies; as loyal wife, faithful to her husband's memory; and as loving mother, sublime in her self-abnegation. As Adolf Schaeffer noted, this queen, in her prudence, courage, and virtue, soars high above the male figures in the drama. To her, Tirso gives his most beautiful thoughts and whole poetic inspiration.

174 Kohler, E., and M.-A. Crusem. "L'extraordinaire fortune d'un thème littéraire: Inés de Castro ou La Reine Morte." Bulletin de la Faculté des Lettres, Strasbourg, 35 (1957), 372 82.
As in legend, so in literature, Inés is always given the place of honor, even to the detriment of Pedro. Throughout all the literary variations on the theme, the figure of Inés remains unchanged. While radiating sweetness and beauty, she symbolizes the eternal struggle between feelings and duty, and the inevitable expiation of the woman who allows herself to be carried away by a love that, although shared, is forbidden.

175 Laborde, Elena Beatriz. "La figura femenina en la obra dramática de Lope de Vega." Boletín de Literaturas Hispánicas, Rosario, Argentine Republic, no. 8 (1969), pp. 65-83.
Laborde comments on several examples from Lope's varied repertory of feminine characters, who are created with love and painted with imagination, humanity, and poetry. In most of his plays we see a woman, under the guardianship and vigilance of father or brother, whom the power of love obligates to rebellion and independence. This independence is manifested in very different ways in Lope's works. His female characters, of diverse social classes, environments, and states of life, are perhaps the most exact representatives of the Spanish women of his time.

176 LaGrone, Gregory G. "Salas Barbadillo and the Celestina." HR, 9 (October 1941), 440-58.
The Celestina type, a favorite with Salas, appears regularly in his satirical sketches. Examples include the two Celestinas of La hija de Celestina; Elena's mother and her dueña. The description of the mother constitutes a character sketch rather than an exact copy, but it does retain the spirit and many traits of the original. Nevertheless, the material concerning the mother is simply an intercalated story in the novel's plot, something that is not true of

the dueña Méndez, who has an important role in molding the heroine's character. To Salas, all dueñas are Celestinas, and his description of them is always colored by his recollection of Rojas's character. A third Celestina type is Celia of the novela in tercets, "La Madre," intercalated in the 1614 edition of La hija de Celestina. She illustrates only one aspect of Celestina's character, her venality. Elena herself in many ways parallels Rojas's Areusa.

The character Emerenciana of the novelettes "El escarmiento del viejo verde" and "La niña de los embustes," published in Corrección de vicios, is Celestina come back to life; while the Comedia de la escuela de Celestina y el hidalgo presumido, presents a Celestina who ascends to a professorial chair toward the beginning of each of the three acts, in order to propound her teachings.

177 Lanuza, José Luis. Las brujas de Cervantes. Buenos Aires: Academia Argentina de Letras, 1973. See especially pp. 19-37.

Although the Quixote lacks this typical character of Spanish literature, scenes of magic or witchcraft abound in Cervantes's other works, so that one can speak of Cervantes's witches, just as one can speak of Shakespeare's or Goethe's. Cañizares of El coloquio de los perros is the best described of them all.

178 Lara, M. V. de. "María de Zayas y Sotomayor." BHS, 9 (January 1932), 31-37.

Zayas's feminist ideas are a bitter complaint about the situation of women in Spain. They are not a defense of rights, but of woman herself. Zayas offers pictures which accurately reflect the reality of domestic and feminine life in a century when both seem to have been of very secondary importance.

179 Laurenti, Joseph L. "La feminidad en la Segunda parte de la vida de Lazarillo de Tormes, de Juan de Luna." RL, 22, nos. 43-44 (1962), 71-74.

Luna insists on the darkest colors in depicting women. He dehumanizes them by caricature, and delights in presenting their sensual nature in a grotesque and horrendous manner. This author, who seems to have been guided by the models of La Celestina and Delicado's La Lozana andaluza, gives us one of the most vigorous chapters in antifeminist literature of all times.

180 Lavroff, Ellen C. "Who Is Rosaura? Another Look at La vida es sueño." Revue des Langues Vivantes, 42 (1976), 482-96.

Calderón's Rosaura must be discussed under the double aspect of her human and her theological identity. On a human level, her development parallels Segismundo's, and he helps her to regain her honor. During the play she is a monstruo like Segismundo, appearing in three different sexual roles: male, female, and a combination of the two. Her sexual identity cannot be established until her honor is restored by marriage to Astolfo. On a theological level, Rosaura represents divine grace, and she helps Segismundo redeem himself.

181 Lazo, Raimundo. "Algunos retoques a la crítica de La gitanilla." BACL, 1 (1952), 370-83.
Preciosa is a complex cluster of reflections including the real or human, and the ideal and artistic. Other feminine characters of Cervantes who might be considered analogous do not show the same admirable equilibrium of reality and ideality that defines the whole being of Preciosa. Her conduct is exemplary but never impossible.

182 Leavitt, Sturgis E. "A Maligned Character in Lope's El mejor alcalde el rey." BCom, 6 (Fall 1954), 1-3.
Feliciana has not been fully understood by critics who have labeled her hateful or abject. The main reason for her presence in the play is to provide the semblance of an explanation for Tello's delay in raping Elvira. Feliciana knows her brother well enough to realize she can do nothing by opposing him directly, so she pretends to side with him and plays for time.

183 _____. "Strip-Tease in Golden Age Drama." HRM, I, 305-10.
Leavitt studies plays in which female characters appear medio desnudas. Cervantes seems to be the first to use this theatrical device, in Los baños de Argel. Rojas uses it most often, even though in the majority of cases there is little justification for it. Moreto provides only one, but the most provocative example, in El desdén con el desdén.

184 Lentzen, Manfred. "Alcina, Armida und die Jüdin von Toledo: Drei Verführerinnen bei Ariost, Tasso und Lope de Vega." SLGZ, pp. 229-68.
The love story of Alfonso VIII and the Jewess of Toledo, as told in the nineteenth book of Lope's epic poem Jerusalén conquistada, exhibits parallels with Ariosto's Alcina episode and Tasso's story of Armida. Although Lope differs from the Italians in that he speaks only generally of Raquel's beauty rather than describing it in detail, he, like them, presents a woman who, through her beauty, is capable of keeping a

Christian hero from his duty. Raquel, however, does not resemble an enchantress, as Alcina does, nor a diabolical temptress, like Armida. She is a symbol of a tragic love, a Jewish woman who must be sacrificed in order to guarantee the security of the nation.

Lope treats the same topic in the *comedia*, *Las paces de los reyes y judía de Toledo*. Since he is concerned to show that Spanish unity must be grounded on the observance of the monarchical order, which in turn is based on the Catholic faith, Lope has Raquel become a Christian shortly before her death.

185 León, María Teresa. "Algo sobre la verdadera Dulcinea del Toboso." *Revista Nacional de Cultura*, Caracas, 22, nos. 140-41 (1960), 90-108.

Dulcinea is the axis of the *Quixote*. She has been called the symbol of love, glory, fame, and fatherland, and she is all of these. She is also the synthesis of all the Spanish village girls whom Cervantes ever saw in his duties as *alcabalero*.

186 Levisi, Margarita. "La crueldad en los *Desengaños amorosos* de María de Zayas." *Estudios literarios*, pp. 446-56.

With a single exception, all Zayas's stories contain at least one episode of physical cruelty exercised by a male member of the family upon the protagonist. The cruelty is hyperbolized because of the author's vehement feminism. The heroines are presented as saints and martyrs who, betrayed by human love, suffer and die animated by divine love. Death sometimes surprises them in gestures similar to those which art attributes to Christian martyrs.

187 Lida de Malkiel, María Rosa. "La dama como obra maestra de Dios." *Romance Philology*, 28 (February 1975), 267-324.

The motif arose as a theological reflection, as part of the admiration before all creation as the work of God. In this context woman's beauty arouses, not direct praise, but praise of the Creator. María Rosa Lida gives examples from Spanish literature of later variants of the motif, in which the scales are often tipped on the side of the creature, and Nature is often substituted for God as artificer. Perhaps the most frequent variant is that of God or Nature creating the beautiful lady as a demonstration or example of his/her power or wisdom.

Also discussed in this article are related motifs which originated in poetic Platonism. Sixteenth-century poets use these themes but imitate as well the Latin poets Horace, Virgil, and Ovid, whose ideas of love and therefore of the lady are radically different. The motifs which endure in Spain are those based firmly on the Biblical attitude. On the other hand, an example of one which took no root in Spain, is that of the beloved lady created by God in order to attract men to Himself through her beauty.

188 _____. Dido en la literatura española: Su retrato y defensa. London: Tamesis, 1974.

An epigram of Ausonius provides the Renaissance and later generations of writers with the figure of Dido as exemplar of unhappiness, as well as a model of beauty. Virgil's Dido also inspires many works, the most celebrated of the tragedies being Guillén de Castro's Dido y Eneas. No scene from the Virgilian episode awakened such an echo as that in which Dido sees Aeneas sailing out to sea. Another motif, that of Dido's death by Aeneas's sword, became the ideal pattern for the frequent aggrieved women in the Spanish theater. Curiously lacking in popularity is the motif of Dido's desire for a son by Aeneas; only Lope poetizes this circumstance.

Another version of the legend of Dido, anterior to the Virgilian, which knows nothing of her love affair with Aeneas and presents her as a model of chastity and firmeza, flourishes during the Golden Age. There are numerous protests against the Aeneid's calumny of Queen Dido, and she becomes an important referent in the literary genre of feminine defense, with respect to both woman's intellectual capacity and her moral responsibility. In Antonio de Torquemada's Coloquio pastoril, for instance, Dido is the only example that the antifeminist interlocutor cannot gainsay. Cristóbal de Virués's Tragedia de Elisa Dido makes the personality of the protagonist stand out in singular fashion. It presents her faced with a moral conflict, the choice between saving her city and maintaining her purpose of widowhood. Gabriel Lobo Lasso de la Vega's La honra de Dido restaurada expresses the more typical Spanish attitude, since it is more a polemic directed against the falsity of the Aeneid than a work of art about the non-Virgilian Dido.

If the "historical" Dido provokes sympathy as an example of chastity, the Virgilian figure is exempted from moral responsibility by many Spanish writers. This clearly implies an essential falsification of the Aeneid, but in Golden Age theater responsibility in cases of honor is reserved for the man, and the pair of Dido and Aeneas falls into the conventional scheme as burlada and burlador. The extreme form of this conception, in which the heroine is reduced to the passivity of an object, is romance 487 of

Durán, which depicts as fainting and inert, that woman who in Virgil, dominates the indecisive personality of Aeneas.
Another theme in vogue in Golden Age literature, the list of inventors, includes numerous women and exalts Dido as queen and foundress. Nevertheless, this myth is rare when compared with references to her as a model of chastity or fidelity in love.

189 _____. "Dido y su defensa en la literatura española." Revista de Filología Hispánica, 4 (July-September 1942), 209-52.
The subject matter is included in the author's book Dido en la literatura española: Su retrato y defensa.

190 _____. "Para la génesis del Auto de la Sibila Casandra." Estudios de literatura española y comparada. Buenos Aires: EUDEBA, 1966, pp. 157-72.
The sibyl of Gil Vicente's auto, by her pride (she believes herself to be the prophesied Virgin who will give birth to the Messiah) and her humiliation, dramatically illustrates a verse from the Magnificat. The Spanish dramatist not only totally humanizes his sibyl, dissipating her sinister supernatural aura, but also eliminates her eternal condemnation by showing her repentant and imploring the intercession of the Virgin.

191 Lins, Ivan Monteiro de Barros. Lope de Vega 1562-1635. Rio de Janeiro: J. R. de Oliveira, 1935. See pp. 153-64.
Nearly all of Lope's comedias contain allusions tending to the exaltation of women. One, El premio del bien hablar, is exclusively dedicated to this end. For Lope the role of woman is to be beautiful, discreet, and virtuous; not a warrior or a scholar. A woman should be given a certain independence, such as the freedom to choose her own husband and a sense of her own responsibility for guarding her honor.

192 López Caballero, Alberto. "El tema Fedra en la literatura." Razón y Fe, 170 (1964), 425-38.
The author touches briefly on Lope's El castigo sin venganza. Lope dramatizes the process of "Fedra's" falling in love, which until then had simply been narrated. He also has "Hipólito" fall in love with "Fedra," an innovation inconceivable for the classical tradition.

193 López Estrada, Francisco. "Tradiciones andaluzas: La leyenda de la morica garrida de Antequera en la poesía y en la historia." ArH, 28, nos. 88-89 (1958), 141-231.
The author examines different versions of the episode

of the mora garrida in the Coplas de Antequera and its relationship with other forms and poetic themes. Like the women of the serranillas, the Mooress initiates the game of love and is a woman of masculine spirit (as shown by her throwing down from the walls a Moor who shot an arrow at the Christian knight). There are also resemblances with the canciones de mal-maridada. In France these poems mock the deceived husband, but in Spain the unfaithful wife asks the husband to punish her with death, as she deserves. There abound in Spanish lyric poetry restless malcasadas who do not receive from their husbands the treatment they hoped for, and who fill the songs with nostalgic complaints of their loss of freedom. They are from all the social classes, and their declarations range from spiritual expression of refined sorrow, to vulgar imprecations.

The Mooress is to be criticized for her evil intention with respect to her Moorish husband, whom she wants killed so as to give herself more freely to her new love. In contrast, the prose version, which insists on the Mooress's desire to convert to Christianity, describes her as a lady of radiant beauty, with whom the Christian falls in love simply through contemplating her.

194 López Morales, Humberto. "Celestina y Eritrea: La huella de la tragicomedia en el teatro de Enzina." La Celestina y su contorno, pp. 315-23.

In the figure of Eritrea of the Egloga de Plácida y Vitoriano, the incredible richness of Celestina has been reduced to a few basic lines. Although both take pride in their professional skills, Eritrea's major one is that of midwife, which is not taken from Celestina, while the theme of alcahuetería, so important in the earlier work, is absent from the eclogue. Both women are old and poor, but Eritrea shows no nostalgia for her lost physical beauty nor depression over the pleasure that will never return, as Celestina does. Eritrea is a celestinesque type without any individualization. At times she takes on the outlines of a figura bufa, intended only to obtain an easy laughter.

195 Loud, Mary. "Tirso's Comic Masterpiece: Marta la piadosa." Hispanófila Especial, no. 1 (1974), pp. 81-94.

It is a misconception to see Marta as a female Tartuffe, and to read the play as a character study in hypocrisy. Instead of Marta's being herself the focus of mockery, she is principally the agent who devises schemes to ridicule and confound her father and Urbina, the true comic characters. Her temporary descent to their level serves a special purpose. In showing us that even his heroine has flaws, Tirso is trying to establish the brotherhood in folly of all mankind.

196 Lowe, Jennifer. Cervantes: Two novelas ejemplares. La gitanilla, La ilustre fregona. Critical Guides to Spanish Texts, 2. London: Tamesis Books, 1971.

Though an objective assessment leads us to appreciate Preciosa's character and realize its exemplarity, she may be somewhat too sentimentalized for our taste. For readers of the time, however, she would be a vast improvement on the Italianate shepherdesses or distraught damsels so often encountered in novels; as well as more aesthetically pleasing than most female characters of the picaresque genre.

Costanza has the same virtues as Preciosa, and in her case, too, the ultimate revelation of her real identity and social status is to be considered a tribute to and proof of the way in which she has behaved. Yet, she is really a rather negative sort of character in the sense that she is virtuous because she refuses to get involved. She in undeniably exemplary but not as satisfying an artistic creation as Preciosa.

197 Lundelius, Ruth. "Tirso's View of Women in El burlador de Sevilla." BCom, 27 (Spring 1975), 5-14.

The ignominious characterization, incontinence, and consequent radical censure of these women disprove the view that Tirso was an unqualified champion of women. At the same time, they furnish a significant instance of his general outlook on the feminine sex, which, if profoundly pessimistic, was rather commonplace among educated clerics of his time. Tirso considerably diversifies the moral weaknesses of the women in El burlador. In the process he exhibits a number of traditional exemplars of the errant woman: the inordinately proud and disdainful, the irresponsible rebel against paternal authority, the incontinent flouter of precepts of church and state, and the foolish social climber. These women are "virtuous"; yet regardless of their social status they are uniformly portrayed as literally helpless in resisting their desires. The ending does not illustrate any extravagant advocacy of woman, but rather justice, with perhaps gant advocacy of woman, but rather justice, with perhaps a dash of compassion. Humbled and presumably wiser, the women are harmoniously integrated into their proper function in nature and society--marriage.

198 Lloréns, Washington. Dos mujeres del Quijote: La mujer de Sancho, Maritornes. San Juan, Puerto Rico: n.p., 1964.

Also in Boletín de la Academia de Artes y Ciencias de Puerto Rico, 2 (1966), 53-76.
Teresa Panza is not such a zafia aldeana as she is often made out to be; she is not immune to contagion by the quixotic spirit. Her reaction to the letter she receives from the Duchess reveals her passage from reality to illusion, doubt to credulity, common sense to the sentido quijotesco.
Maritornes is a generous figure, charitable and compassionate, with the charming candor of a student in a school for young ladies. Vulgarly happy, she rights during the day, the errors of her nights.

199 Llorens Castillo, Vicente. "Un episodio del Quijote: La aventura de la hermosa morisca." RdA, 7 (1946), 25-32.
Ana Félix of Part II, Chapter sixty-three of the Quixote resembles Venus in the divine quality of her beauty and in her emergence from the sea; but as a Christian woman, not a pagan deity, she represents beauty sublimated by sorrow. Her pure love and beauty triumph over hatred, dogma, and the razón de estado. Dulcinea, the inspiration for Don Quixote's feats and the personification of glory and fame, lacks true efficacy for the new bourgeois world. The only eternal feminine who can dignify it is Ana Félix, who links the bitter experience of injustice to purest innocence.

200 Lloris, Manuel. "El casamiento engañoso." Hispano, no. 39 (May 1970), pp. 15-20.
Cervantes's doña Estefanía is a character in need of vindication. It is evident that she seeks anxiously to redeem herself through marriage and tries desperately to win the good will and affection of Campuzano. She is no Magdalen; she is a sinner well aware of the inconveniences of sin, and she is moved, not by moral compulsions, but by a strong desire to become respectable, a part of stable society. If this possibility is denied her, she will renew her irregular life, reluctantly but not with repugnance. Campuzano simplifies and falsifies her conduct, reducing it to a level with his own. The story is, above all, that of the tragic-grotesque attempt of an unhappy woman in search of social redemption.

201 Mackey, Mary. "Rhetoric and Characterization in Don Quixote." HR, 42 (Winter 1974), 51-66.
The article contrasts Don Quixote and Marcela as they reveal themselves through their speeches in Part I, Chapters two and fourteen. They communicate their character by the rhetorical conventions they use and do not use. Marcela is an example of didactic oratory which manifests classical

restraint. Her purpose is to communicate with her audience, not to dazzle or confound.

202 Maldonado, Felipe C. R. "Quevedo y sus caricaturas de la mujer." *EstLit*, no. 538 (April 15, 1974), pp. 10-11.
Maldonado discusses types of women in Quevedo's *Sueños*, including *busconas* and prostitutes, adulteresses, *dueñas*, *viejas presumidas*, enamoured nuns, involuntary virgins, and the hypocritically devout. What he especially criticizes in all these feminine professions and states of life is hypocrisy. In his rejection of the sublimation of woman which characterized the Renaissance, Quevedo is conscious of his own hyperbole. His are the logical reactions of a recalcitrant bachelor of the seventeenth century, who was, nevertheless, a subject of Venus and who must have been influenced by his childhood experiences of growing up in a household of women.

203 Marasso, Arturo. *Cervantes: La invención del Quijote*. Buenos Aires: Biblioteca Nueva, 1943.
Marasso includes sections on female figures from the *Quixote*, whom he compares to classical ones. For example, Marcela resembles in her fierceness the shepherdess Camila of Virgil's *Aeneid*; the Duchess recalls Dido in the moment when the latter departs for the hunt; and Altisidora pretends to be a new Dido, scorned and deserted by the new Aeneas Don Quixote.

204 Márquez Villanueva, Francisco. "Dorotea, la muchacha de Osuna." *ArH*, 46, nos. 141-46 (1967), 147-63.
Dorotea is one of the best figures of the whole *Quixote*, a type of woman who attracts everyone's sympathies and admiration. She is an unusually capable woman, and one of moral delicacy, but primarily she is a woman in love. Too clever to be seduced and too energetic to be forced, she gives herself to Fernando of her own free will because she is in love with him from the first. Deep inside she is persuaded that she merits him, and in the end her discretion achieves what her bodily charms did not. Dorotea's character is determined by her *despejo*, natural elegance, and especially, valor. She maintains a virile attitude in the face of misfortune, uniting in herself the best of both sexes. She embodies the Renaissance ideal of the *virago* in the noblest sense of the word. She also symbolizes the triumph of sanctified love over lasciviousness, though not in the manner of an *exemplum*. Her conduct is a practical argument which affirms her right to realize fully, in body and soul, the destiny of her femininity.

205 _____. "Los joyeles de Felismena." *RLC*, 52 (April-December 1978), 267-78.

Montemayor uses the lapidary tradition and iconological language to say something about the nature and worth of the character Felismena, whom he wishes to proclaim as *señora* of the *Diana*. Her virtues include constancy--in contrast to Diana's inconstancy, loving loyalty, loftiness of thought, and above all, heroic hope. She shows perfect love by working actively for the happiness of her beloved, who is in love with another lady.

206 _____. *Personajes y temas del Quijote*. Madrid: Taurus, 1975.

This book includes sections on Dorotea, Leandra, and Zoraida. The treatment of Dorotea is basically the same as in the author's "Dorotea, la muchacha de Osuna." He adds that Dorotea, who begins by incarnating the literary type of the *mujer vestida de hombre*, goes on to play the archaic role of the *doncella menesterosa*, which she can do precisely because she is a woman of great spirit and very much in command of herself.

The case of Leandra, which is very similar to the Italian poem "Leandra" by Pietro Durante da Gualdo, is a typical misogynistic episode within the great thematic repertory of the *Quixote*.

Zoraida is not meant to be an exemplary paradigm. Her actions manifest her *sangre fría* and her gifts as a consummate actress. She venerates, above all, herself reflected in Lela Marién and turns her back on the reality of the most sacred human ties. Even her name, which means "Pleiades," connotes distance and coldness as well as beauty.

207 Marquina, Rafael. "Tres mujeres del *Quijote*." *Revista Cubana*, 22 (1947), 138-56.

Quiteria the beautiful is also Quiteria the passionate and *lista*. She exhibits this last quality perhaps more than any other person in the book, including Dorotea. At the decisive moment she intuits Basilio's plan, through her love, integrity of character, and nobility of feeling; and with modesty and composure she cooperates with him.

Marcela incarnates the prototype of the pastoral heroine according to the criterion of Cervantes. As a woman who has embraced her will completely, she is a contrast to the falsity of the shepherdesses of other works, who are submissive to a law of fatality. She is ahead of her time in her vindication of liberty in loving and not loving.

Maritornes manifests a kind of elemental animality, which impels her as much to pious and kindly as to "sinful" or cruel actions. Yet there is in her subconsciousness, a voluntary exercise of the act of selection, for she struggles in Don Quixote's arms.

208 Mas, Amédée. La caricature de la femme, du mariage et de l'amour dans l'oeuvre de Quevedo. Paris: Ediciones Hispano-Americanas, 1957. See especially pp. 11-84.

Quevedo's misogyny, which is built on an inclination toward women, is summed up in his formula demonios de buen sabor. Beneath the two masks, equally false, of woman's bodily charms and of artifice, Quevedo as philosopher and moralist, discerns the horror and repugnancy of our origins and biological condition. He caricatures both physical aspects and moral qualities of women. One of his obsessions is the theme of the old woman, in whom all the faults of her sex are accumulated to an extreme degree. Some female types characteristic of Quevedo's gallery are more specific types of the old woman, such as the dueña, whose most singular trait is the general and violent hatred or aversion which she inspires; the bruja and hechicera; and the huéspeda. Other types, not tyrannized by old age, are the fregona, invariably Galician or Asturian, who represents for Quevedo the lowest level of woman; the verdulera; the culta and discreta, different from the entendida, a feminine ideal; the monja, treated relatively kindly; the beata, portrayed in the satirical works as a hypocrite who covers lubricity with the cloak of religion; and the doncella, in whom authentic virginity is virtually nonexistent. When Quevedo praises a woman, it is for being in some way like a man.

209 Matulka, Barbara. "The Feminist Theme in the Drama of the Siglo de Oro." RR, 26 (July-September 1935), 191-231.

The feminist theme is introduced early in Spanish drama, as exemplified in Encina's Egloga de tres pastores, and constitutes the central theme of a whole cluster of plays. Their main character, the man-hating beauty who militantly sets out to avenge the wrongs of women, becomes a fixed convention. The theme takes a milder form in plays in which the woman is jealous of her own liberty, after having seen the misery to which so many loving women are subjected. Nearly all the plays take up the age-old controversy over the superiority of men or women and over the specific merits and defects of the sexes.

The comedia almost invariably metes out defeat to the feminist heroine, who is relegated in the end to domestic duties, the obligations of love, self-sacrifice, and marriage. The feminist conflict is usually waged within the women themselves, and they are the ones who justify their change of attitude. Their reasons emerge, the dramatist implies, from the very nature of woman, and are evoked by the demands of the social order. In this respect the comedia's feminism differs from preceding manifestations, where the main conflict was a debate between man and woman, a bloody issue left unsolved between unreconciled adversaries.

210 Mayberry, Nancy K. "The Fate of Aldonza in Part III of Tirso's Santa Juana Trilogy." Hispanófila Especial, no. 2 (1975), pp. 73-77.

It is a commonplace in Golden Age drama that the ending of a play finds all dishonored maidens avenged, married, or banished to the convent. However, in the Santa Juana trilogy one woman, Aldonza, remains unavenged, unmarried, and with no mention of her final fate. In this respect Aldonza resembles Tisbea of El burlador de Sevilla, and like Tisbea she has sinned through hubris.

211 _____. "On the Structure of Tirso's Santa Juana Trilogy." South Atlantic Bulletin, 41, no. 2 (May 1976), 13-21.

The three plays correspond to the three stages in Juana's spiritual journey to perfection: the purgative, illuminative, and unitive ways. Juana is a saintly figure from the beginning; her one great mental conflict resulting from her doubts over having used male clothing for her escape to the convent.

212 _____. "The Role of the Warrior Women in Amazonas en las Indias." BCom, 29 (Spring 1977), 38-44.

Although the Amazons' role is subordinate to that of the tragic character Gonzalo Pizarro, they have three important functions in this Tirsean play. They are symbolic of the utopia of the past, serve as prophetic commentators on the action, and reveal character, specifically, Gonzalo's tragic flaw.

213 Mazzara, Richard A. "Saint-Amant's 'L'Andromède' and Lope de Vega's 'La Andrómeda'." KRQ, 8 (1961), 7-14.

Unlike the heroine of the French poem, Lope's Andrómeda has as active a role in the dialogue as the hero, Perseus. She is fully conscious during the latter's struggle with the monster and, in a sense, takes an active part in it. She needs no mother or confidante to assure her in the end of what is rightfully hers.

214 Mendeloff, Henry. "The Maritornes Episode (DQ: I, 16): A Cervantine Bedroom Farce." RomN, 16 (Spring 1975), 753-59.

Unlike Casalduero (see entry 57), Mendeloff does not believe Maritornes should be interpreted allegorically, nor does he agree with Ziomek that she exhibits profound human traits. She must be seen as Cervantes describes her; a burlesque character, ugly and grotesque.

215 Monge, Félix. "La Dorotea de Lope de Vega." Vox Romanica, 16, no. 1 (January-June 1957), 60-145.

The fusion of the typological with the individual in the characters can be seen most clearly in Dorotea. She strives to play the role of the dama of the comedia, a role created for her by her poet lover. She succeeds in great measure, but underneath there is a more authentic personality which manifests itself whenever she has to confront situations that are not at all literary. The Dorotea who astonishes one with her rhetoric when speaking to don Bela or writing letters to Fernando, is very different from the woman of flesh and blood who dialogues with Gerarda or argues with her mother. Dorotea, who represents Lope's first love, Elena Osorio, is, poetically speaking, the most deeply felt character in the work.

Marfisa's intervention in the action is slight but leaves a strong and favorable impression on the reader. Her conduct and expression are marked by a serene nobility and spirit of self-abnegation. Being free of any literary contagion, she sees objectively. The ironic observations which occasionally escape her are the result of an earlier desengaño. Marfisa is enveloped by an emotion which is the most genuinely human in the entire work. Even when she knows herself to be spurned by her former lover, she continues loving and giving with the same intensity as before.

Gerarda is a very original creation of Lope's; one of the most perfect of his literary characters. She differs profoundly from Celestina, her antecedent. Completely lacking in solemnity, she is a conscious personification of frivolity. In reality she is a decorative figure, for there is nothing in the work which could not have happened without her intervention. She is a comadre, the final term of the progressive Castilianization of the go-between. An element that separates her decisively from any of her forerunners is her comicality. Although she is also an experienced and astute woman who knows how to use situations for her own advantage, she gives the impression of lacking, at bottom, prudence and balance. Allusions to her witchcraft are more a tribute to the tradition of the type than a real statement about Gerarda. She shares with Celestina the trait of avarice, but in Gerarda it is much less rigid and tragic, more accurately described as shameless and importune begging. Whereas Celestina controls whatever situation she encounters up to the moment of her death, Gerarda never does. Lastly, unlike Celestina, she has an elemental religiosity, which leads her in the end to desengaño and repentance.

216 Monner Sans, R. Las mujeres de Alarcón. Buenos Aires: n.p., 1916.

We know, superficially, that the woman created by Lope was passionate and affectionate; Tirso's, more given to pranks and stratagems; Calderón's, lofty, proud, and almost always unhappy. Tirso studied woman in books, not in the confessional, as was once supposed. The others were in direct contact with women.

Alarcón, who must have had a quite imperfect acquaintance with women because of his physical deformity, neither exalts nor derides them. Without penetrating very deeply into the feminine mode of being, he portrays women as they are; sometimes tender and sweet, other times mischievous and playful, astute and egotistical, or noble and upright. He delights in the depiction of the praiseworthy woman more than of her opposite.

217 Montero, Lázaro. "Dulcinea." ACer, 9 (1961-62), 229-46.

The name Dulcinea has a very distant relationship, if any, with that of Aldonza, and the supposed Aldonza has even less relationship with Dulcinea. Other writers, such as Avellaneda, who use Cervantes's work as a point of departure, have not understood Dulcinea because they stubbornly insist on seeing her through Aldonza and forget that she is entirely the creation of Don Quixote. Dulcinea, the most imprecise aspect of a very ambiguous book, has been considered the symbol of glory (Unamuno), liberty (André Suarés), Poetry (Suarés), and Spain (Ramón y Cajal). Montero agrees most with the last interpretation.

218 Montiel, Isidoro. "La belleza en las mujeres de Cervantes." BBMP, 23 (1947), 219-26.

The text of this article repeats the ideas of Cotarelo y Valledor (see entry 74).

219 Moore, Roger. "Leonor's Role in El esclavo del demonio." RCEH, 3 (Spring 1979), 275-86.

The link between the two main plots and the secondary plot of Mira de Amescua's play is the thematic contrast between obedience and disobedience, the former exemplified in the character Leonor. Her role on stage is twofold: to contrast with Lisarda and to exemplify the dutiful daughter.

Her chief characteristic, absolute obedience to her father's will, is established from the start when she calls herself his slave.

Moore believes, differently from Valbuena Prat (*see* entry 337), that Leonor's role is clearly not insignificant; she shows no signs of hypocrisy; she is capable of noble actions, including heroic obedience; she does not deliberately toy with her lovers, except in one regrettable incident, of which she repents immediately; and she does not opportunistically choose the more powerful man, since she has no choice in the matter of whom she marries.

*220 Morales Oliver, Luis. *Dulcinea del Toboso*. Madrid: Barbero, 1960.

221 Morel-Fatio, Alfred. "*La prudence chez la femme*: Drame historique de Tirso de Molina." *Etudes sur l'Espagne*. Third Series. Vol. 3. Paris: E. Bouillon, 1904, pp. 25-72.

Tirso's María de Molina is fundamentally the queen of history or of the chronicle, a beautiful mixture of strength, valor, and informed prudence. She is a Castilian matron with Roman sentiments.

222 Morley, S. Griswold, and Courtney Bruerton. "Lope de Vega, Celia, y *Los Comendadores de Córdoba*." *NRFH*, 6, no. 1 (1952), 57-68.

Morley and Bruerton disagree with María Goyri de Menéndez Pidal's view (see entry 136), that "Celia" and "Lucinda" are the same woman, Micaela de Luján. "Celia" could be a poetic name which served to group various emotional crises experienced by Lope with more than one woman. The physical description of Celia is not really unique but could well be a type of feminine beauty.

223 Mortier, Roland. "Libertinage littéraire et tensions sociales dans la littérature de L'Ancien Régime: De la 'pícara' à la 'fille de joie'." *RLC*, 46 (January-March 1972), 35-45.

López de Ubeda's Justina is a pícara only by reason of the unstable character of her existence and because she does not integrate herself in the conventional feminine career pattern. She is an astute but prudent young woman who aspires to social stability in marriage. She is distinct from the protagonist of Salas Barbadillo's *La hija de la Celestina*, who is a veritable criminal. In a *roman libertin* such as *La pícara Justina* there is no resort to crime, since this would compromise irremediably the heroine's reintegration in the social order.

224 Motta Salas, Julián. "Dulcinea o el amor de Don Quijote." Universidad de Antioquía, 22 (1948), 249-74.

Cervantes exalted woman in the immortal figure of Dulcinea, while Avellaneda, through the same figure, stained the ermine mantle which woman's honor should be.

225 Mujica, Barbara Kaminar. "Tragic Elements in Calderón's La dama duende." KRQ, 16 (1969), 303-28.

Angela, the protagonist of the comedy, is a tragic character in the sense that she is both victim and perpetuator of the social code of honor. Like the heroes Segismundo and Eusebio of La vida es sueño and La devoción de la cruz, Angela is a self-willed, determined person who is alienated from society and involved in a desperate search for her own identity. Instead of rebelling openly like them, however, she, as a woman, must maintain her decorum and manipulate her destiny through cunning. Since her goal is basically freedom, not love, the real issue remains unresolved with her marriage to Manuel.

226 _____. "Violence in the Pastoral Novel from Sannazaro to Cervantes." Hispano-Italic Studies, no. 1 (1976), pp. 39-55.

Diana and Alcida of Gil Polo's Diana enamorada represent two extremes with regard to love. Diana believes that human beings are the victims of their emotions, while Alcida tries to obviate emotion and live by reason alone. Both women, however, view love as a force that engenders suffering and psychological or even physical violence. This attitude is less mature than that of Marcelio, who incarnates a combination of reason and emotion coupled with an understanding of the mutability of fortune.

227 Murray, Janet Horowitz. "Lope through the Looking-Glass: Metaphor and Meaning in El castigo sin venganza." BHS, 56 (January 1979), 17-29.

It is surprising that Casandra was formerly considered the tragic heroine of the play, since she alone ignores her relationship to God and is totally grounded in the temporal and practical realm. She is a ruthless, shrewd, and passionate woman, committed not to love but to vengeance. She is not internally torn, but given totally to her desires. Throughout the play she is a symbol not of her own destruction and dishonor, but that of others. The most important cluster of metaphors associated with her is the sea, storm, and tempest. She is a sirena and evil sea-witch, who lures Federico to his death.

Contrasts are set up between Casandra and Aurora. The former is a false light, a blaze which inspires heat and rashness; Aurora is a penetrating light, ultimately the light of rebirth. Casandra is the inspirer of the Icarus in man; Aurora represents the Daedalian spirit of reason.

228 MacCurdy, Raymond R. "The Bathing Nude in Golden Age Drama." RomN, 1 (November 1959), 36-39.

Baroque dramatists and poets make abundant use of voluptuous word-pictures of the bathing nude. Lope sets the pattern for subsequent encounters of the bathing nude and admiring male in Las paces de los reyes y judía de Toledo. The theme reaches artistic maturity with Góngora's Fábula de Polifemo y Galatea. In most of the later plays the bathing nude serves the purposes of romantic comedy rather than tragedy, and the encounter is no longer dramatized but related by way of exposition. Rojas Zorrilla especially exploits the theme, his most provocative example being found in Esto es hecho. As in the case of courtly love, it is the beauty of the woman perceived through the eyes that arouses the passion and desire of the male. After being brought into contact with the lady in this way, the galán must undergo a period of servitude to prove himself worthy of possessing her through marriage.

229 _____. "On the Uses of the Rape of Lucrecia." Estudios literarios, pp. 297-308.

Among the uses of the Lucretia story in Spanish Golden Age literature are: (1) Lucretia as symbol of chastity, constancy, and fortitude; (2) the story as a subject for tragedies; (3) Lucretia and her story as a source of evocation or as an analogue in plays; (4) the affective qualities of her death as a subject of poetry; and (5) Lucretia as symbol of foolishness. Encina's Egloga de tres pastores offers an example of the first use. In Rojas Zorrilla's Lucrecia y Tarquino, the heroine takes excessive pride in her own virtue and has an unconscious desire to experience a martyr's beautiful death. Lope de Vega alludes to Lucretia in more than fifty plays, usually in order to invest certain characters with the qualities of the chaste matron or her lustful ravisher. From the affective point of view, serious poets on the whole regard Lucretia's suicide as an exemplary and heroic act. Examples are Juan de Arguijo's sonnet and Manuel de Gallego's silva on the theme. In the Baroque period, celebrated women of antiquity become the victims of the skepticism of the age, Lucretia among them. Alonso de Castillo Solórzano's "A la necia muerte de Lucrecia" and Quevedo's "Consulta el rey Tarquino" illustrate her new role as example of putaísmo and necedad.

230 ______. "Women and Sexual Love in the Plays of Rojas Zorrilla: Tradition and Innovation." Hispania, 62 (May-September 1979), 255-65.

One of the characteristic manifestations of Rojas's feminism is the independent spirit of his women, which moves them to react critically, and often defiantly, against parental coercion in matters of love and marriage. Another, and the one on which Rojas's reputation as a champion of women's rights chiefly rests, is the refusal of some of his heroines to accept the double standard with respect to the honor code. Progne y Filomena constitutes the severest challenge to this double standard to be found in Golden Age theater. Moreover, a few of Rojas's women assert their equality with men in spiritual and intellectual endowments.

These three factors, then, tell us something about women's dissatisfaction with and response to some of the social attitudes and practices of their age, including male domination. They should not, however, lead us to think that Rojas's heroines are ultra-liberationists or women who want nothing to do with men. On the contrary, the hallmark of this dramatist's women is a free and contagious voluptuousness which they freely express and enjoy. In spite of his feminism, Rojas was not above exploiting the female body in order to titillate his audience, nor was he above cultivating a kind of machismo by portraying women overcome with passion at the sight of a handsome man. Nevertheless, most of his women are not impassioned nymphs but rather purposeful beings who choose deliberately to follow love's dictates because they are convinced love is the supreme joy. Regarding sexual love as an end in itself and having no thought of future children, their abiding care is how to win and keep their men, a care they share with most women of other Golden Age dramatists. Recitals of the intimacies of the nuptial bed are given alike by women who welcome their partners' desire and by those forced into unwanted marriages. In the anguished lament of Leonor of La traición busca el castigo, Rojas succeeds in adopting a woman's point of view, something rare in the Golden Age. La vida en el ataúd strikingly combines sexual love and feminism, Aglaes being the most voluptuous and aggressive of all Rojas's heroines. Thus freedom in love does not mean for these women merely the right to choose one's marital partner, but also the right to heed the call of sexual love, in or out of marriage.

231 McGaha, Michael D. "The Sources and Meaning of the Grisóstomo-Marcela Episode in the 1605 Quijote." AC, 16 (1977), 33-69.

Cervantes establishes parallels between Marcela and the mythological figures of Daphne, Hippolytus, and Eurydice, all of whom are essentially negative, though not altogether unsympathetic. Their association with the moon is conferred by Cervantes on Marcela, who, incomplete and imperfect without Grisóstomo, needs him as the moon needs the sun, as the world-soul needs the intellect, or as the natural appetites need the regulation of wisdom. Just as the moon is eclipsed by the shadow of the earth, Marcela allows her selfish desire for freedom to come between her and Grisóstomo.

Both Don Quixote's longing for the Golden Age and Marcela's withdrawal into an unreal pastoral world are actually a desire to escape from freedom and the responsibility it entails into the security of instinctive behavior. Both characters strive to attain the state of nature through mechanical imitation of unreal artistic creations.

St. Ambrose's De Virginibus, which seems to have influenced Cervantes, emphatically urged virgins to avoid appearing in public. Marcela decided to play at being a shepherdess in opposition to the desires of her guardian and the townspeople. She was playing with fire, and her reprehensible behavior contrasted with the just and holy intention of her suitors, who are justified in calling her cruel and ungrateful. The speech which she delivers from the top of the rock is inappropriately timed, arrogant and self-serving; completely lacking in humanity and respect for the man who killed himself out of love for her. The arguments by which she affirms her blamelessness are invalid. Since she freely chose to leave her uncle's house, live in the country, and frequent the company of men, she cannot escape responsibility for the consequences of her actions. If she truly desired solitude and retirement, she could have remained at home or entered a convent. She offers but one statement, and that tacked on as an afterthought, which indicates that her way of life is motivated by anything other than willfullness and hedonism.

232 McGrady, Donald. "Notes on Jerónima de Burgos in the Life and Work of Lope de Vega." HR, 40 (Autumn 1972), 428-41.

The Celestina-like figure, Gerarda in La Dorotea, is a caricature of Jerónima de Burgos. Parallels drawn between the two are their converso origins, obesity, avariciousness, lasciviousness, and fondness for sorcery and wine. Moreover, Lope elsewhere refers to Jerónima as "la señora Gerarda."

233 McKay, Carol L. "María de Zayas: Feminist Awareness in Seventeenth-Century Spain." Studies in Language and Literature: The Proceedings of the 23rd Mountain Interstate Foreign Language Conference. Edited by Charles L. Nelson. Richmond,

Kentucky: Eastern Kentucky University Press, 1976, pp. 377-81.

María de Zayas seems to have been the first to incorporate feminist ideas into Spanish works for leisure reading. Challenging the current opinion of her time that women were designing, weak-minded creatures of very unstable morals, she imputes women's illiteracy to the fear and envy of men, and accuses them of deliberately deceiving women. She maintains that it is the innocent woman who suffers, since it is virtually impossible to please a husband.

However, Zayas also berates women for allowing men to deceive them and to get away with it. She incites women to rise above the current immorality and regain their previous self-esteem. Two stories that exemplify two of her most frequently expressed ideas are "El juez de su causa," which contends that women can achieve in the world as well as, or better than, men, and "El prevenido engañado," which underlines the need for women to be educated.

234 McKendrick, Melveena. "The Bandolera of Golden-Age Drama: A Symbol of Feminist Revolt." BHS, 46 (January 1969), 1-20.

McKendrick discusses variations on this manifestation of the mujer varonil in such dramatists as Lope de Vega, who provides the prototype; Vélez de Guevara, in whose La serrana de la Vera we find the most overtly masculine woman in the Spanish theater; Mira de Amescua; Tirso de Molina; Calderón de la Barca; and Agustín Moreto. The female bandit rebels against an essentially masculine society and the unjust social conventions imposed upon her sex by men. Since, according to the honor code, the wronged woman cannot really win, she resorts to crime in an attempt to meet unreason in kind. The bandolera's rebellion is, above all, an attempt to become the arbiter of her own destiny. In general, the dramatists sympathize with the female rebel, insofar as they allow her to repent at the end. Her revolts are condemned, but her need to revolt is understood and sympathized with.

235 _____. "The 'mujer esquiva'--a Measure of the Feminist Sympathies of Seventeenth-Century Spanish Dramatists." HR, 40 (Spring 1972), 162-97.

The mujer esquiva, by far the most popular of the many variations of the mujer varonil in Spanish Golden Age drama, is a woman who for some reason is averse to the idea of love and marriage; as a natural outcome she is usually but not invariably averse to men as well. The type is central to the whole theme of feminism in the Golden Age theater, because more than any other, she illustrates the exact nature of the seventeenth-century attitude toward women. The treatment accorded her reveals how far dramatists were ready to go in the defense of women. In the eyes of these playwrights, hers is a revolt against nature, and she must eventually be led, or driven, back to the path of sanity and true happiness. Not one of these women remains voluntarily single, not even in doña Ana Caro's El conde Partinuplés, the only play in which a woman presents a mujer esquiva.

There can be no worthwhile motives behind a woman's esquivez, only a moral fault. This is usually either vanity, in which case the treatment is lighthearted, or arrogant pride, in which it is more serious. With respect to plays involving the former motive, Lope's Los milagros del desprecio created a genre, which culminated in Moreto's El desdén con el desdén. The most important of the plays involving the motive of pride is Lope's La moza de cántaro. It could be called the thesis play on this subject, the thesis being that the desire for independence and the impulse to unnecessary self-assertion is improper in a woman.

Another group of plays falls outside the main body in that the heroines' motives are not strictly vanity or pride. Of these, Ricardo de Turia's La belígera española presents a female protagonist who identifies with the opposite sex in order to avoid becoming weak and effeminate. Her essential character does not change, but in the end she can accept the fact that she is a remarkable woman and that her qualities are not alien to femininity. She accepts a man, not as lord and master, but as an equal.

The mujer esquiva of Golden Age drama is not so much an extension of the literary theme of feminism, as a reaction against a contemporary aspect of feminism which was, within a restricted circle, very much alive.

236 _____. Rev. of The Invisible Mistress: Aspects of Feminism and Fantasy in the Golden Age, by Frederick A. de Armas. MLR, 73 (July 1978), 672-75.

McKendrick disagrees with Armas in the interpretation of the heroine of Calderón's La dama duende. Angela is not dependent upon her brothers because she is a widow but because she is a bankrupt widow. The lines in which Honig (see entry 159) detects incestuous desires are probably provoked by bitterness at her financial dependence. Angela is less a magus, manipulating reality for irresponsible and unnecessary ends, than a life-starved human being, clutching ingeniously at every straw of excitement that comes her way. She does not mistakenly seek to flee the paradise of her own home, but rather escapes from a prison into a match that is, by any standards, a desirable one.

237 _____. *Woman and Society in the Spanish Drama of the Golden Age: A Study of the "mujer varonil"*. Cambridge, England: Cambridge University Press, 1974.

Among the types of *mujer varonil* treated are, in their order of popularity during the Golden Age; the *mujer esquiva*, the *bandolera*, the warrior, the *bella cazadora*, the scholar or career woman, the avenger, and the amazon. Lope established the *mujer varonil* as a stock character and remained its greatest exponent. The only important dramatist who ignored the type was Alarcón. The later manifestations of the *mujer varonil* are not morally degenerate but simply artistically inferior creations. It is doubtful that, as Ashcom contends (*see* entry 23), the Lesbian motif is implicit in most plots involving masculine women. *Varonil* in the Golden Age was invariably a term of praise, as much when used of women as of men. The *mujer varonil*'s revolt is against society and convention, and women's inferior position therein, not against her sexual role vis-à-vis man.

Besides according with the seventeenth-century fondness for extremes of personality, the type had the basic attraction of a dream. For women theatergoers, she provided vicarious freedom and adventure; for men, the appeal was sexual. The heroines' final stance also satisfied masculine pride and the male conquering instinct.

Although Cueva and Virués are truer feminists in an absolute sense, they wrote as if the battle for sexual equality were already over, whereas Lope and later dramatists realized it had barely begun and thus, made a potentially greater contribution to the progress of the feminist cause. No one before the seventeenth-century dramatists had really explored woman's position in relation to the society in which she lived. They are liberal without being revolutionary, and can be broadly described as prepared to uphold woman against Society but never against Nature. A woman's place is by the side of a man, but as long as she remains there she can be allowed her female integrity and dignity.

Lope is more intensely concerned with the life and rights of woman than any other dramatist, but he is also her sternest judge and, more than all the others, sees her as a sexual being. Tirso's understanding of female psychology is subtler than Lope's, and his tolerance of female independence and eccentricity, greater. His greatest service to women is to allow them a high degree of intelligence, which other dramatists tend to ignore or underrate. Calderón's tendency to transcend sex in the investigation of profoundly human themes, indicates a true belief in woman's spiritual equality. Moreto's *No puede ser* presents the only truly emancipated woman of the Golden Age.

238 Nagy, Edward. *Lope de Vega y la Celestina: Perspectiva seudocelestinesca en comedias de Lope*. Veracruz: Universidad Veracruzana, 1968.

The old women--mothers, aunts, *dueñas*--in Lope's plays may resemble the Celestina of Rojas and even be called second Celestinas, but they are similar to her only in superficial ways. Their purpose is to amuse, and their character can be described as pseudo-celestinesque. This type, who appears from time to time in Lope, does not possess the demoniacal power of the original but is rather like a comic figure in an *entremés*. The dramatic role of the procuress is invariably reduced to the necessary minimum. The overriding passions and basic motives of the prototype, such as egotism and greed, lose their independent and decisive character, coexisting with several others. In the presence of the pseudo-celestinesque character, the propensities to *tercería* inherent to the servant types are more visible and vitalized, while the *celestina* herself is diminished and even degraded, often becoming the butt of the *criado*'s *burlas*. Celestina loses her authority.

A study of several examples of the type in Lope reveals that they are *celestinas sui generis*, without rigid attributes. They include Fabia of *El caballero de Olmedo*, Teodora of *El galán Castrucho*, Marcela of *La bella malmaridada*, Dorista of *La francesilla*, and Belisa of *El amante agradecido*.

Besides the *vieja celestinesca*, there is sometimes present in Lope's *comedias*, a *criada* in whom celestinesque elements are accumulated and concentrated. These threaten her status as *criada* but do not make her a strong *celestina* type.

239 Navarro de Adriaensens, José María. "Los personajes femeninos en el *Burlador* de Tirso de Molina." *RJ*, 11 (1960), 376-96.

Humor and a sense of responsibility are the strongest human traits in Tirso's feminine characters. In some plays, such as *El burlador de Sevilla*, woman is not officially the protagonist but a decisive element in balancing the action. Woman in this play is not so much the antagonist of don Juan as his natural complement. Each of the duped women makes definitive use of her free will and is at fault to some extent. Each has a distinct personality as well as a distinct social situation. Isabela schemes; Tisbea flirts; Ana fights; and Aminta, an ambitious village girl, falls through naiveté and rises without feeling the blow overmuch.

Tirso's continual preoccupation with woman and her human and moral problems revolves around the questions of honor, marriage without love, and above all, the responsibility of woman and a society of stereotyped norms.

240 Navarro González, Alberto. "Dulcinea y Galatea." Homenaje a Arturo Marasso (1890-1970). Cuadernos del Sur. Bahía Blanca: Panzini Hermanos S.A.C.I., 1972, pp. 127-32.

Galatea is a first attempt at portraying the sublime figure of Dulcinea. Both are outstanding for gifts of nature and virtue, more than for those of fortune. Both are called peerless (several of the same phrases are applied to them by their knight and shepherd), and both inspire a very lofty type of love. Catalina de Salazar, Cervantes's wife, must have been an influence in the creation of these two figures.

241 Nichols, Geraldine Cleary. "The Rehabilitation of the Duke of Ferrara." Journal of Hispanic Philology, 1 (1977), 209-30.

It is difficult to comprehend why the Casandra of Lope's El castigo sin venganza has been regarded as such a wronged innocent, since she is characterized by a series of mythological and classical images which are overwhelmingly negative. She is Circe and siren, both of whom lure men to their death, while Circe also metamorphoses her victims into animals. She is Helen, whose beauty occasions the destruction of a kingdom; the Trojan horse; and Casandra, the prophetess whose dire predictions are never heeded. Her principal role in Ferrara is that of genetrix, not helpmeet, as she herself admits. At first she wears the mask of martyred wife, but later she enters into the affair with Federico quite conscious of its perversity. She becomes a traitor by virtue of profaning her lord's name and bed and thus, deserves her death.

242 Nichols, Madaline. "A Study in the Golden Age." Estudios hispánicos, pp. 457-76.

In a study based on more than fifty novelas cortesanas, including those by María de Zayas, Nichols attempts to recreate the social history of the time, with considerable space devoted to various aspects of the life and customs of women.

243 Nieto, Ramón. "Cuatro parejas en el Quijote." CHA, no. 276 (June 1973), pp. 496-527.

Nieto discusses Dorotea, Luscinda, Zoraida, and Clara de Viedma with respect to their character and personality, as well as the socioeconomic factors that influence them. Dorotea, who surpasses all other Baroque literary heroines, should not deceive us with her apparent candidness; her manner is not that of a wounded dove but of a humiliated lioness. Beautiful and sensual, ambitious and with a head full of fantasies, she is furious over what Fernando has done to her and what is being said of her in the village. She goes to the mountains strong and ready to fight, not to lament and withdraw from the world, but to plan vengeance. Luscinda, all of whose actions fit conservative molds, lacks options. When she obeys, she is morally subject; when she disobeys, she becomes physically subject. She is weak and docile, and saved only by chance. Zoraida is the most inconsistent and false character of the whole book. Her conversion and fanatic devotion to Christianity are not convincing. It is doubtful that she who has been unfaithful as Mooress and daughter will be faithful as Christian and wife.

244 O'Connor, Thomas Austin. "La desmitificación de Celestina en _El encanto es la hermosura_ de Salazar y Torres." _La Celestina y su contorno_, pp. 339-45.
The play has an excellent celestinesque characterization, although there are great differences between this Celestina and her archetype. Whereas Rojas's Celestina combines formidable talents with diabolical power, Salazar's figure uses simply the natural arms of _argucia_ and _astucia_. She seems more a promoter of delight and manipulator of passion than a servant of hell.

245 Oliver Asín, Jaime. "La hija de Agi Morato en la obra de Cervantes." _BRAE_, 27 (October 1947-April 1948), 245-339.
Zahara, protagonist of _Los baños de Argel_, and Zoraida, from the tale of the Captive in _Don Quixote_, are based on the same historical figure. Both are heroines of a love story as well, yet there is an abyss between them.

246 Oñate, María del Pilar. _El feminismo en la literatura española_. Madrid: Espasa-Calpe, 1938. See Chs. 4 and 5.
To the feminist polemic, which continues to discuss the moral character of women, the Renaissance brings new themes, such as woman's intellectual capacity. Those who ignore this last topic include both detractors and defenders of women. Among those who do discuss the subject are Cristóbal de Acosta, who believes women's lesser capacity is due to a lack of education, not a lack of ability; Juan Luis Vives, who says a woman should be encouraged to study if she shows an aptitude for it but that her learning should be imparted to her family alone; and Huarte de Sant Juan, in whose view women are physiologically incapable of intellectual activity. Indeed most authors of the period deny the intellectual capacity of women. The traditional ideal of the woman consecrated exclusively to her home finds its definitive

expression in Luis de León's La perfecta casada. St. Teresa's position is not easy to specify precisely. Some of her opinions, such as those on woman's natural weakness, seem antifeminist when judged superficially. She also speaks, however, of women's heroism, of the fact that Christ judges differently from other men, and of women's right to cultura, though this must not be used in a vainglorious way.

In the seventeenth century the themes of the feminist debate are basically the same as those of the sixteenth, but now woman emerges in defense of her sex. The theater on the whole contributes negatively to the intellectual evaluation of woman by presenting a caricature of the erudite type; depicting learning as incompatible with beauty; and preaching that common sense suffices for women, since the only problems they must solve are related to the home. The theater does, however, affirm woman's right to choose her own spouse and moves gradually toward the conclusion that woman is her own best guardian. Moreover, despite the dominant opinion, there are hints that manual tasks do not suffice to occupy women and that education is a way to combat frivolity. Among the more antifeminist writers are Góngora, Quevedo, and Gracián. In the picaresque novel women are an element in the pícaro's globally pessimistic view. On the other side, feminism owes Cervantes the categoric affirmation of woman's personality.

247 Pabon, Thomas. "Secular Resurrection through Marriage in Cervantes' La señora Cornelia, Las dos doncellas and La fuerza de la sangre." ACer, 16 (1977), 109-24.

Virtue and honor are, for seventeenth-century women, the two poles around which life revolves; that is, they serve as the given context for the emotional content of almost every novela. In the three works mentioned in the title, women are placed in a variety of situations which force them to restore and fulfill themselves through marriage. Cervantes changes the traditional story of the knight who rescues the damsel in distress; for the most part, women must rescue themselves and win through to a marriage which satisfies not only the heart and soul, but also society. In this respect Cervantes's women are always acting in a way perfectly in accord with their natures.

248 Palacín Iglesias, Gregorio B. En torno al Quijote: Ensayo de interpretación y crítica. Second Edition. Madrid: Ediciones Leira, 1965. See pp. 176-80.

Dulcinea exists only in Don Quixote's imagination, but his own creation becomes for him a necessary illusion, an inspiration and guide in his endeavors. Besides being a

Palacín

conventional figure, Dulcinea is a symbol, inseparable ultimately from what she symbolizes: love, goodness, and the illusion which keeps hope alive. She is not fundamentally different from Petrarch's Laura or Herrera's Leonor, although in the case of these there is more insistence on the real sensorial image, and in that of Dulcinea, on the imaginative and intellectual elements.

249 _____. "La moza labradora en quien encarnó Dulcinea del Toboso." Hispano, no. 33 (May 1968), pp. 7-15.
In Dulcinea there were two personalities: the ideal dama and the moza labradora. The former was created by Don Quixote's imagination, but the other, for knowledge of whom we must listen to Sancho, doubtless had a real, historical existence.

250 Palls, Byron P. "Una justificación del título de la comedia de Mira de Amescua La fénix de Salamanca." Hispano, no. 47 (January 1973), pp. 59-71.
Just as the mythical phoenix of antiquity was a bisexual creature, so in the play doña Mencía wears male garb. She evokes a reaction characteristically shown toward men, and conducts herself in an aggressive, warrior-like fashion, desirous of proving her masculinity. Moreover, she acts, up to a point, as a trotaconventos and could thus be called by analogy, a priestess of Venus; the phoenix being considered a priest of the same goddess.

251 Paoli, Roberto. "Auerbach e Dulcinea." Il Bimestre, Florence, Italy (November-December 1969), pp. 2-8.
Theoretically there are as many Dulcineas as there are characters who invoke her, but in practice they can be reduced to two: that of Don Quixote and the Antidulcinea of Sancho. In the episode commented by Auerbach the least important element is Sancho's attempt to deceive his master; the woman he presents is really his own Dulcinea. We do not have here a confrontation between realism and the conventional idealism of Don Quixote, but rather a grotesqueness which is likewise linked to literary conventions. Sancho's Dulcinea descends from the same line as Maritornes, though there is some difference between them. Both proceed from the traditional jocose vein of the Middle Ages and Renaissance and are, basically, the serranas of the Arcipreste de Hita.

252 Parker, Alexander A. "Santos y bandoleros en el teatro español del Siglo de Oro." Arbor, 13, nos. 43-44 (July-August 1949), 395-416.

Women are the first protagonists of the theme announced in the title of this article. Lope's La serrana de la Vera presents the theme in its simplest form. After the serrana is deceived and seduced by a man who abandons her, she, being conscious of her innocence, affirms her own dignity as a woman by avenging herself on the society which scorns and rejects her. Two outcomes for the serrana-bandolera are pardon by the king and marriage to the man who deceived her (Lope), or condemnation and execution (Vélez de Guevara). In the second and more typical phase of the theme's development, the heroine ends as a penitent (Mira de Amescua) or even a saint (Tirso de Molina).

253 Parker, Jack H. "La monja alférez, de Juan Pérez de Montalván: Comedia americana del siglo XVII." Actas del Tercer Congreso, pp. 665-71.
Montalván's play can be called an imaginative presentation of several aspects of Catalina de Erauso's life as a soldier. The richest and most nuanced of the play's characters, she does not possess the seductiveness of attractive femininity, but rather the ferocity of an excessively masculine character. Like Lope, Montalván knew the feminine heart. In this play he succeeds in showing in it a certain inquietude, desire for freedom, and ambition for adventure. He also portrays in Catalina, love for country and great religious fervor. Carmen Bravo-Villasante (see entry 44) sees the protagonist as abnormal and caricatured, but others find her a legitimate product of the times, and always heroic.

254 Paz Aspe, María. "Teresa de Jesús o la superación de la feminidad." Estudios de historia, literatura y arte hispánicos ofrecidos a Rodrigo A. Molina. Edited by Wayne H. Finke. Madrid: Insula, 1977, pp. 39-43.
Teresa, knowing that men would be the definitive judges of her writings, wrote in language that would please them. Thus, for example, she points out the dangers for women in the spiritual life, such as the illusions of the imagination, and speaks often of women's flaqueza and torpeza. On the other hand, she expresses the conviction that in the spiritual life the nun is equal to the friar and even affirms that women advance more in the spiritual life. Her humanity is above the man-woman polarization, but on occasion she is obliged to point it out and comment upon it.

255 Peltzer, Federico. El amor, creación en la novela (Beatriz-Dulcinea-Justina). Buenos Aires: Columba, 1971. See pp. 105-62.

Whereas the Middle Ages idealized woman to an extreme, the Renaissance continues to praise her but is no longer her slave. Don Quixote restores the scepter to woman because he is anachronistic. Cervantes, on the other hand, is tolerant.

Dulcinea is woman in the abstract and lives by Don Quixote's creation, while Aldonza continues to exist repressed in his memory. There is a progressive purification of Dulcinea, who is not an object but a moving force, and whose mission is to give breath and spirit to Don Quixote once he has given her life. Although he renounces the name and identity of Don Quixote at the hour of death, he does not renounce Dulcinea.

256 Pemán, José María. "Belisa, la melindrosa." EstLit, no. 241 (15 May 1962), p. 3.

Lope is the Spanish dramatist who best knows women. In his feminine figures we do not confront homogeneous psychologies oriented toward a single passion or virtue, as in Tirso's María de Molina or Shakespeare's Lady Macbeth, but the desconcierto of feminine reality. Los melindres de Belisa is one of the most discerning and advanced studies of women in Golden Age theater, in which Lope deals with the psychosomatically upset heroine with the impertinence of a psychologist and the impassivity of a doctor.

257 Pérez, Luis C. "Coplas desconocidas del tema celestinesco." HRM, 2, pp. 51-57.

The coplas included in this article are an example of a kind of imitation of La Celestina which was popular in the sixteenth century. The procuress differs from her prototype in being more of a trickster than a professional concerned to fulfill her contracted duty. Like her predecessor, she is the victim of an unjust society, which has given her an inferior role, and she is obliged to use her astuteness in order to live.

258 Pérez de Guzmán, Juan. "Bajo los Austrias: La mujer española en la Minerva literaria castellana." La España Moderna, Madrid, 114 (1898), 50-79.

Various male writers of the Golden Age mention with praise or publish the works of contemporary women writers or women of culture and learning. Vicente Espinel is the first to individualize women of superior ingenio in his Casa de la Memoria, although he mentions only those with a superlative reputation in the art of music and song. Juan Pérez de Montalván cites in Para todos only a few of the illustrious women writers of the period, including María de Zayas, whom he calls "décima musa de nuestro siglo." Lope mentions several women in the Laurel de Apolo but still gives no idea of the degree of participation by the feminine element in Golden Age literature. Pedro de Espinosa, in the first part of Flores de poetas ilustres de España, concedes, for the first time, a place of honor to women by inserting their productions among those of the greatest ingenios of his time. The women are doña Cristobalina Fernández de Alarcón, from Antequera; and doñas Hipólita and Luciana de Narváez, from Granada.

259 Pérez Navarro, Francisco. "El diablo en Occidente: En torno a la Celestina, a la Cañizares y a la madre del buscón don Pablos." Indice de Artes y Letras, Madrid, 13, no. 126 (1959), 19.

Whereas Rojas's Celestina was an hechicera rather than a true bruja, (since she was not the devil's submissive servant but rather tried to use him for her own ends and even to deceive him) la Cañizares of Cervantes's Coloquio de los perros and Aldonza Saturno de Rebollo, Pablos' mother in Quevedo's Buscón, were indeed [black] witches in the proper sense of the word.

260 Perry, T. Anthony. "Ideal Love and Human Reality in Montemayor's La Diana." PMLA, 84 (March 1969), 227-34.

Diana, who is not admitted to the Temple of Diana, because of her infidelity to Sireno, represents a fallen ideal. Felismena does not act out of pure selflessness. It is more than plausible that she subconsciously desires Felis's unfaithfulness, thus making her love impossible of fulfillment and so proving her heroic fidelity. Belisa is a psychologically dense character. Egocentric and detached from reality, she symbolically murders her beloved, and her very being becomes identified in her own eyes with her heroic, extravagant despair. Up to now no one has offered an interpretation of Felicia.

261 Petriconi, Helmut. "El tema de Lucrecia y Virginia." Clavileño, 2, no. 8 (1951), 1-5.

The basic plot of Livy's stories of Lucretia and Virginia concerns the shame inflicted upon a woman by the sovereign or his lieutenant which spurs a political revolution. The theme is present in Tirso's El burlador de Sevilla, both Lope's and Calderón's El alcalde de Zalamea, and Lope's Peribáñez and Fuenteovejuna. Lope's works present a contradiction, in that the female victim involved is a labradora, who traditionally had no honor to lose.

262 _____. "Trotaconventos, Celestina, Gerarda." Die Neueren Sprachen, 32 (1924), 232-39.
Gerarda, the most important secondary character in Lope's La Dorotea, outdoes Celestina in her hypocrisy and sanctimoniousness, but the scenes in which the inebriated Gerarda frankly relates her early life leave no doubt that she is Celestina, as determined by her own time and milieu. Her controlling trait is still the basest greed, in the service of which she enlists all the resources of her cunning and knowledge of human nature.

263 Peyton, Myron A. "La discreta enamorada as an Example of Dimensional Development in the Comedia." Hispania, 40 (May 1957), 154-62.
In this play Lope creates one of his rare mother roles, although Belisa's characterization is greatly exaggerated. Whereas the lady in the Boccaccian tale which served as Lope's source, possesses no introspection, Fenisa is both actor and contemplator or judge of her actions. Force of will is the strongest positive characteristic in the female protagonists. Fenisa is richly endowed with it, along with the traits of openness of character and frank sensuality. Her resolution is not merely directed to the execution of a feminine stratagem, as in Boccaccio, but is the basis of valentía.

264 Pierce, Frank. "La gitanilla: A Tale of High Romance." BHS, 54 (October 1977), 283-95.
Cervantes's Preciosa, presented from the beginning in hyperbolic terms, is a paragon among her people and an ornament among all women. She is conceived as immune to environmental influences and as possessing a very special grace. A complex creature who is both gypsy and not gypsy, she emerges as almost a personification of Christian virtues and marriage. It is she who directs Andrés and also acts as his savior at the critical moment.

265 Placer, Gumersindo. "Algo sobre las monjas en las comedias de Tirso de Molina." Estudios, 16, no. 49 (1960), 319-30.
Generally speaking, Tirso's texts pertaining to convent life and nuns manifest concessions to popular taste. Although we see sanctity, we also see the same human passions and failings as in other groups of society.

266 _____. "Mari-Hernández la gallega--Notas para un prólogo." Grial: Revista Gallega de Cultura, 40 (1973), 171-86.
Tirso succeeds in making the protagonist of this play a mirror of the feminine youth of Galicia. He depicts

her as a good daughter and friend, a staunch patriot, a pious Christian, strong in work, rich in love, noble in sentiment, and firm in decision.

267 Poblet, Fernando. "En torno a Maritornes." *EstLit*, no. 367 (8 April 1967), p. 38.

Cervantes's Maritornes, the literary character most badly treated by critics, was not a vulgar *buscona* but rather a *bruja* in physical appearance, with a strong sexual drive.

268 Prado de Arai, Emma. *Dulcinea, protagonista invisible del Quijote*. Tuxtla Gutiérrez, Chiapas, México: Ediciones Arte y Letras, 1947.

Dulcinea is the most important moral authority in the novel and, as such, the most important character. She is a decisive element in the novel's structure since she is not simply an occasional factor but a constant spiritual presence who gives poetic depth to the work. Her function is not to figure visibly in public but to establish the destiny of the other principal characters by serving as the invisible force which moves and directs them. She represents what is most real and true for Don Quixote. Her image, unlike his other fantasies, is never confused with some other figure, precisely because she is not a momentary presence but the *alpha* and *omega* of his life.

269 Quirarte, Clotilde E. *Personajes de Juan Ruiz de Alarcón*. México: El Libro Español, 1939. See pp. 55-112.

Alarcón traces his feminine figures with weak strokes, probably because of a lack of familiarity with women, due to his deformity. Among the twenty-four works used in this study, there appear six feminine types of first rank, of whom two are outstanding: Celia, the maid in *Las paredes oyen*, and Jimena of *Los pechos privilegiados*, a secondary character but the most beautiful feminine model created by Alarcón. His *enamoradas* are not characterized by passionate seizures and energetic impulses, but suffer a discreet torment. Diana of *El dueño de las estrellas* is the feminine figure of most valiant integrity in Alarcón's theater. If parsimonious in giving beauty of spirit to his ladies, Alarcón is gallant in always giving them a husband.

270 Ratto, Luis Alberto. "La edad de la mujer en las *Novelas ejemplares*." *Mercurio Peruano*, Lima, 30 (1949), 506-18.

Fixing the age of his feminine protagonists seems to be an indispensable device in Cervantes's novelistic technique. The ideal of beauty-virtue is incarnated in heroines between fourteen and eighteen years of age. The combination evil-ugliness, in contrast, does not have specified age limits, the age issue not being terribly important here, unless there is an attempt to point out more clearly the opposition between evil and virtue in characters of similar age. Whereas Cervantes's young women are passive, suffering or awaiting masculine action, his women of maturer age are active and usually dissolute. It seems that the ideal cannot be fully obtained except in the privileged springtime of life. Cervantes establishes a progressive gradation of sin and deformity, portraying in la Pipota and la Cañizares all the lascivious women of the novelas in their old age.

271 Rauhut, Franz. "Consideraciones sociológicas sobre La Gitanilla y otras novelas cervantinas." ACer, 3 (1953), 145-60.
Cervantes does not mold Preciosa as a superhuman miracle but as an ideal character within reality. He gives her something of the gypsy nature of her environment, yet not so much as to taint her inner nobility.
Leocadia of La fuerza de la sangre is a psychologically unsatisfactory character for the modern reader. Completely dominated by the aristocratic mentality and its attitude toward honor, she manages inexplicably to overcome her strong disdain for her seducer and to conceive a heartfelt love for him.

272 Reig, Carola. "Doña Ana Girón de Rebolledo, musa y editora de Boscán." Escorial, 15, no. 45 (1944), 289-302.
It is only through Boscán's verses that we discover the image of his wife. In the "Epístola a D. Diego Hurtado de Mendoza," she appears as both inspiring muse and woman of flesh and blood. Her suavidad and dulzura above all make Boscán's life a true paradise.

273 Remos, Juan J. "Dulcinea y Altisidora." Anales de la Academia Nacional de Artes y Letras de Cuba, 27 (1947-48), 27-46. Also in the author's Ensayos literarios. Madrid: Talleres Gráficos Aro, 1957, pp. 39-50.
Dulcinea, symbol of the ideal, is the synthesis of all man's preoccupations about the enjoyment of the vision of God. She has her counterpoint in Altisidora, who embodies all that woman possesses of the seductress by her external beauty and proverbial sagacity. These two figures constitute in Cervantes's work the two powers which struggle in man's heart, determining the quality of his destiny as one or the other gains ascendancy.

274 Rey Caballero, José María del. La mujer sevillana en la obra de Lope de Vega. Seville: Imprenta Municipal, 1975.
Woman occupies first place in Lope's productions, and

the sevillanas have in the totality of his work a place of preeminence and preference. Rey Caballero treats eleven specific feminine characters, mostly drawn from the comedias. Dorotea of La Niña de plata, a compendium of virtues and perfections, personifies Lope's adoration of Seville.

275 Reynolds, Winston A. "Hernán Cortés y las mujeres: Vida y poesía." NRFH, 18, nos. 3-4 (1965-66), 417-35.
Gaspar de Avila's play El valeroso español y primero de su casa portrays Juana de Zúñiga, Cortés's second wife, in whom the dramatist is more interested for her willful character than in Cortés himself. In the anonymous Comedia de los pleytos she is somewhat more feminine, something like a new Ximena. Doña Marina appears in epic poems, such as Gabriel Lobo Lasso de la Vega's Cortés valeroso y Mexicana and Antonio de Saavedra Guzmán's El peregrino indiano, as the Spaniard's loyal interpreter and nothing more, although they do depict her as extraordinary for an Indian woman.

276 Ricciardelli, Michael. "Spanish Imitators of Sannazaro's Arcadia: A Re-evaluation." PPNCFL, 17, no. 1 (1964), 60-66.
It was Montemayor who introduced women into the Arcadian setting. In Gil Polo, his misogyny is converted into a defense of women and accusation of men.

277 Ríos, Blanca de los. "Las mujeres de Tirso." Del Siglo de Oro. Madrid: Bernardo Rodríguez, 1910, pp. 229-75.
The critic controverts the idea that Tirso always painted women as "livianas, inconstantes, traviesas, vanas y caprichosas," whereas Lope's were always admirable. She believes the reverse is truer. Woman in all her psychophysical reality and opulent variety entered the theater with Tirso. His feminine characters, at once Spanish and universal, proceed from three main sources: the Bible, chronicles, and contemporary reality. Among the Biblical heroines, Thamar is the most prestigious tragic figure of the Spanish classical theater. Doña María de Molina of La prudencia en la mujer, the glorification of woman in her three highest categories, queen, widow, and mother, is the loftiest theatrical presentation of the feminine sex. Among Tirso's comedies of character, Marta la piadosa presents a protagonist who is the first hypocritical type in modern theater. His villanas, incarnating nearly every region of Spain, are unique in Spanish theater and even in the history of art. One of his most interesting feminine characters is Lucrecia of La fingida Arcadia, a kind of female Quixote.

278 Rivas Sainz, Arturo. Dulcinea. Guadalajara, Mexico: Summa, 1971. See especially pp. 81-160.

Rivas discusses Dulcinea from five points of view: those of Cervantes, Don Quixote, Sancho, other critics, and his own. For Cervantes Dulcinea is both similar to and different from the ladies of the chivalry novels. Don Quixote is sometimes aware of Dulcinea as his own invention, sometimes seduced by it and absorbed in her "reality." Whereas he synthesizes in one woman all the desirable qualities dispersed in others, Sancho substitutes for each quality of the village girl, Aldonza, the opposite for Dulcinea. His description complements Don Quixote's; the Knight stresses the subjective, what Dulcinea is for him, while Sancho emphasizes her sensorial qualities. It is the almost unamimous opinion of critics that Dulcinea is an ideal, but Rivas does not agree. Dulcinea was not an ideal for Don Quixote, and less for Sancho, because she is not something thought but a woman imagined by them, not Woman or Beauty, but a beautiful woman who could be plastically reproduced. She contrasts with all the other women of the Quixote in that they were created in order to act; she, in order to be loved.

279 Roca Franquesa, José M. "Aventurarse perdiendo (Novela de Doña María de Zayas y Sotomayor)." HAG, 2, 401-10.
The protagonist Jacinta, whose soul Zayas presents to us naked, is a type who would have interested Freud.

280 _____. "El cuento popular: 'La mujer casta deseada por su cuñado' a través de nuestra literatura peninsular." Filosofía y Letras: Revista de la Universidad de Oviedo (May-August 1947), pp. 25-63.
The above theme differs from other accounts of persecuted and ultimately vindicated heroines in two ways: (1) the rejected and calumniating suitor is the husband's brother; and (2) the various chastised persecutors are cured by their victim after they have made public confession of their sins, with which the accused woman is restored to honor. The various versions reveal two different endings; her honor once restored, the woman either lives with her husband again or, disillusioned with life in the world, decides to remain in a convent until death. Roca Franquesa discusses two Golden Age versions, one by Juan de Timoneda and the other, undoubtedly the best version of the theme in Spanish literature, María de Zayas y Sotomayor's La perseguida triunfante.

281 _____. "La ideología feminista de doña María de Zayas." Archivum, 26 (1976), 293-311.
Zayas's arguments on the subject of women, like those of most Golden Age writers, are not original. The Renaissance

environment was propitious to the reconsideration of the feminist issue; defense of woman's rights was no longer based only on principles of an emotional or biological nature, but also on theological arguments. The seeds of the feminism developed in the theater and novela of the seventeenth century must be sought in Erasmus and his sixteenth-century disciples. His influence can be seen in such writers as Luis Vives, Juan de Espinosa, Cristóbal de Acosta, and Pedro de Luján.

Zayas's opinions on women revolve around two issues: (1) their equality with men regarding rights and duties in all areas of life, for which reason they must be educated so as not to depend on men completely; and (2) freedom in choosing a husband. At the same time Zayas demands of men respect for and defense of women, even where there is equality of the sexes. An interesting aspect of her feminism is the affirmation that the decadence of a country is due to the corruption of habits in men and the little esteem they have for women.

282 Rodríguez Cepeda, Enrique. "Fuentes y relaciones en La serrana de la Vera." NRFH, 23, no. 1 (1974), 100-11.

Luis Vélez de Guevara's La serrana de la Vera contains a mixture of the primitive and medieval theme of the serrana: the theme of the wild woman who attracts and then kills men, and the theme of the aggrieved woman who becomes a bandolera and avenges herself on men. Rodríguez Cepeda discusses each of these elements as they appear in several comedias of the seventeenth century, in a multitude of variations.

283 _____. "Sentido de los personajes en La serrana de la Vera." Segismundo, nos. 17-18 (1973), pp. 165-96.

In this play Vélez de Guevara opposes a woman's action to a man's words. Gila converts the pastoral and Renaissance elements of sentiment, melancholy, natural feeling, and feminine liberty, into criticism and tragedy. She is the only character who experiences a vital psychological evolution. When she gives in to her father's pleas and begins her womanly transformation, she does so without being forced in any way. There is at work in her a social and moral sufficiency outside the norm. When she later carries out her vengeance after being deceived by don Lucas, she does not wish to defend herself or her cause. Death is her only voluntary solution and is meant by her to be exemplary. She wants all women, and all children who have suffered the rigors of parental domination, to be avenged through her.

284 Rodríguez Gamino, Juan José. "Cervantes y la 'Buena Cristiana'." El Monasterio de Guadalupe, Cáceres, nos. 517-18 (1959), pp. 131-33.

Cervantes's character Zoraida was probably inspired by the miraculous history of a Mooress named Fatima, later Isabel, who came to be called "la Buena Cristiana." There are several coincidences between the two.

285 Rodríguez Guerrero, Ignacio. Tipos delincuentes del Quijote. 2 vols. Quito, Ecuador: Editorial Casa de la Cultura Ecuatoriana, 1966. See I, 1, 6; II, 13, 15.

In Volume I, Chapter one, "La Molinera y la Tolosa," Rodríguez Guerrero comments on various prostitutes and Celestina types found in Spanish literature. He sees in the two prostitutes of the second chapter of the Quixote, women who had become involved in that profession more through necessity and bad example than through any innate tendency to evil. It is possible that Cervantes introduces them at the beginning of his work in order to indicate that the situation in which those unfortunates found themselves constituted the most serious problem in Spain at that time.

Chapter six is entitled "Maritornes." The grotesque description of Maritornes in the Quixote signals a classic case of degeneration and abnormality, the character's exaggerated sexuality being the result of a malfunctioning of the glands. Though she is not a cretin or idiot, she is mentally deficient. Nevertheless, in the depths of her soul there is a certain ingenuous goodness which allows her to overlook the misery in her life. She wins the reader's sympathy by her affability and lack of hypocrisy, hatred, envy, or calculation. On the other hand, she does have certain vices, such as lack of character or of firm convictions, and others which are the almost inevitable result of her ancestry and environment.

Volume II, Chapter thirteen, "La esforzada y no forzada," treats Cervantes's picture in Part II, Chapter forty-five of the Quixote, of a typical buscona, hypocritical and fawning, motivated by greed. Rodríguez Guerrero cites several examples from Golden Age literature which teach that it is well-nigh impossible to force a woman against her will. In this case the very appearance of the woman, her boldness and lack of shame, would make Sancho aware of her imposture.

Chapter fifteen, "Claudia Jerónima," observes that this singular feminine character is Catalan, with the traits peculiar to that people. If a criminal category is to be applied to her, it is unquestionably that of the delincuente pasional. She is a person of irreproachable antecedents and exemplary life, and she loves passionately and totally, like

Shakespeare's Juliet. She is moved to her crime when she believes her honor, a value deeply rooted in her soul through family tradition, to be seriously offended. However, the immediate stimulus is her jealousy, celos imaginarios, the product of her unbalanced temperament. Because she acts under the influence of an uncontrollable psychological upheaval, she is deserving of pity, not punishment or condemnation. She is not an exceptional figure like Queen Isabel, Teresa of Avila, or the Monja Alférez, but an ordinary young woman, in whom it is natural that extreme jealousy should cause such catastrophic effects. Her repentance is evident, even before she discovers the innocence of her victim.

286 Rodríguez-Luis, Julio. "Dulcinea a través de los dos Quijotes." NRFH, 18, nos. 3-4 (1965-66), 378-416.

Dulcinea has little importance for the hero's vital project; she is simply an addition which perfects Don Quixote as a knight errant. The scene in Part II in which the enchanted "Dulcinea" appears on a cart in the ducal palace, underlines by its minimum development Dulcinea's accessory character in the novel, much more marked since the contrast with Aldonza has been left behind. Dulcinea does not in any way have the almost divine function as universal center of love which is assigned to woman in El Cortesano or in the tales of knights errant like Amadís. She is not the ideal, whatever it be, to which Don Quixote aspires. In the deathbed scene it seems as if the Knight's friends believe Dulcinea is essential for his life, but this is an error of perspective. Don Quixote does not even bother to mention her among the elements of the madness which he renounces; the books of chivalry are enough.

287 _____. "Pícaras: The Modal Approach to the Picaresque." Comparative Literature, 31 (Winter 1979), 32-46.

The decline of the picaresque genre in Spain is closely connected with the appearance of the somewhat frivolous pícaras who lead the novel away from any depth of characterization and philosophical preoccupation. Teresa de Manzanares of Castillo Solórzano's La niña de los embustes is probably the best drawn of all Spanish pícaras, yet she is exaggerated and implausible. Nevertheless, although the picaresque novels with feminine protagonists lack the depth of those which treat their male counterparts, the depiction of the pícara's material ambition can lead to relatively powerful character portrayals because of the greed which guides the heroine.

288 Romera-Navarro, M. "Las disfrazadas de varón en la comedia." HR, 2 (October 1934), 269-86.

Although the first comedia in which a woman appears in male garb is Lope de Rueda's Comedia de los engañados, it is Lope de Vega's La Francesilla which presents the figure with the grace and seductiveness that will characterize her in the future. The motives which induce women to don such a disguise are as various as the human passions, but can nearly always be reduced to love. These women represent almost all the social classes but are mostly youthful damas, beautiful and alluring, never hombrunas, although they do display manly spirit. One reason for the popularity of the type was the carefulness and richness with which the character was drawn. It was the gracia of art, not the example of life, which put trousers on Spanish women in the Golden Age theater.

289 Rothe, Arnold. "Padre y familia en el Siglo de Oro." Ibero, 7 (1978), 120-67.

Rothe observes in the course of his article that although Luis de León's La perfecta casada seems extremely conservative to the modern reader (since it presupposes a natural deficiency in woman and thus legitimizes patriarchy in St. Paul's sense) nevertheless, for the readers of that time, the book constituted a re-evaluation of the feminine sex simply because it was a serious work by a theologian and was dedicated to the subject of woman. Moreover, in this work Fray Luis speaks of woman with delicacy; presents her domestic life with affection; recognizes her capacity for formation; her specific qualities; her dignity; and her right to love. Unfortunately, the attempt at a re-evaluation of woman, or rather of the wife, had no possible future due to its Jewish-bourgeois origins.

290 Ruano, P. Nazario de Santa Teresa. La psicología de Santa Teresa: Posturas, feminismo, elegancia. Second edition. México: Editorial Jus., 1955. See especially pp. 176-77, 188-95.

Saint Teresa speaks frequently and in varied tones of the nature of woman. In herself, woman is weak and ignorant, extremely difficult to really know, possessed of a very subtle self-love, and not meant to preoccupy herself with lofty intellectual matters. These judgments spring not from a pessimistic inferiority complex but from an objective evaluation. St. Teresa urges her followers to overcome their natural feminine weakness, affirming that if they do what is within their capacity, the Lord will make them so virile that they will astonish men themselves. The Saint's feminism ultimately transcends analysis by reason of her polyfaceted personality.

291 Rugg, Evelyn. "Two Dramatic Versions of the Ilustre fregona Theme." RomN, 8 (Autumn 1966), 79-85.
Rugg compares the two plays La ilustre fregona y amante al uso (of uncertain authorship although attributed to Lope de Vega), and José de Cañizares's eighteenth-century composition La más ilustre fregona. In both plays Costanza is extraordinarily beautiful and modest, but where in the earlier play she is a noble lady of little individuality, in Cañizares's she is a clever woman with a decidedly daring streak.

292 Ruggerio, Michael J. The Evolution of the Go-Between in Spanish Literature through the Sixteenth Century. Berkeley: University of California Press, 1966. See Ch. V.
The element of witchcraft introduced by Rojas into La Celestina remained as a standard feature in imitations of its "heroine," Delicado's La Lozana andaluza differing from them in this respect. In Feliciano de Silva's Segunda Celestina, the alcahueta hechicera, stripped of covering occupations, becomes a [black] witch who emphasizes her evil contacts and powers; however, this quality must be seen as oriented toward enhancing her professional reputation. She is typical of the imitations of Celestina, who lack the changing facets of personality that make Rojas's character so much more complex and alive.

293 Sáez Piñuela, María José, ed. La moda femenina en la literatura. Madrid: Taurus, 1965. See pp. 10-66.
Sáez Piñuela includes passages from the works of Golden Age writers like Cervantes, Luis de León, and Zabaleta which describe feminine fashions, mostly of the aristocracy or upper class.

294 Salomonski, Eva. "Belisa--Antonia." CHA, nos. 161-62 (May-June 1963), pp. 383-88.
Lope's romance "De pechos sobre una torre" presents an analogy with Dido and Aeneas. Belisa ("Dido") is Lope's wife, Isabel de Urbina; the event, Lope's embarking in the Invencible. Lope shows that he felt Isabel's sorrow; Belisa's complaints are not at all conventional. Her desperation is indicated by her rapid changes of decision. At the same time, throughout the romance she is actually the mouthpiece of Lope himself.

295 Sánchez Rojas, José. Las mujeres de Cervantes. Barcelona: Montaner y Simón, 1916.

The author selects for recollection and reflection certain aspects or qualities of individual women from the Novelas ejemplares, Don Quixote, La Galatea, and Trabajos de Persiles y Sigismunda.

296 Schalk, Fritz. "Lope de Vegas Melindres de Belisa und Bizarrías de Belisa." Studia Iberica: Festschrift für Hans Flasche. Edited by Karl-Hermann Körner and Klaus Rühl. Bern: Francke, 1973, pp. 581-88.

Belisa is, as the basic meaning of the word bizarro implies, beautiful and fascinating, yet she is also characterized by a peculiar, unfathomable caprice. When Lope wrote his Melindres de Belisa, the melindrosa had already become a type through Quiñones de Benavente's Entremés famoso de la melindrosa, from which Lope took several passages verbatim. However, in the figure of Belisa, Lope presents an iridescent form which so fascinated him that he returns to it in a second play. Whereas in the Melindres the heroine's inner conflict is brought to a conciliatory conclusion, in the Bizarrías the tension between Belisa and her surroundings is too great for a reconciliation of the contradictions to be possible. Belisa's caprices, or bizarrías, are an expression of a tendency of Lope's which manifests itself stylistically as well as through the protagonist.

297 Schüler, Gerda. "La culta latiniparla: Lob und Tadel weiblicher Gelehrsamkeit im Siglo de Oro." SLGZ, pp. 440-60.

After discussing in some detail the attitude toward feminine learning in various Golden Age works, the author concludes that, as a whole, the texts treated reveal two contrary tendencies. Writers like Fray Luis de León, Quevedo, Gracián, and Francisco de Zárate believe that education and knowledge contradict the nature and duties of woman. Their arguments are essentially theological in nature and are rooted in the medieval misogynistic literary tradition. Another group of writers, especially Lope de Vega and his disciples, represent the "modern" view that woman is capable of erudition and discretion, and that feminine education and feminine charm are in no way mutually exclusive.

In none of these authors, however, are there any emancipating tendencies in the proper sense of the word. The prevailing conventions are universally respected, and if the boundaries are occasionally overstepped, it is for the exotic appeal involved and in order that custom and decorum be reaffirmed all the more strongly in the end. Thus, Spanish writers lag behind the French in offering a new image of woman. Underlying Spanish literature of the seventeenth century is not only a theological theory of art, but also a theological anthropology. Even those authors who accept feminine learning justify their opinion theologically, appealing to Biblical models. Knowledge in woman has no value in itself but derives its justification through reference to the service of God. Since all earthly goods, material and intellectual, are ephemeral, social transformation, including the emancipation of woman through education, is of only relative value.

298 Sciacca, Michele Federico. "Verdad y sueño en *La vida es sueño* de Calderón de la Barca." *Clavileño*, 1, no. 2 (1950), 1-9.
Rosaura, sensible beauty, awakens the dreaming Segismundo and causes him to enter into eternal beauty.

299 Scott, Nina M. "Honor and Family in *La fuerza de la sangre*." *Studies in Honor of Ruth Lee Kennedy*. Edited by Vern G. Williamsen and A. F. Michael Atlee. Estudios de Hispanófila, 46. Valencia: Artes Gráficas Soler, S. A., 1977, pp. 125-32.
The author remarks in passing that Cervantes's character doña Estefanía is one of the uncommonly strong mother figures in Golden Age literature. A woman of virtue, nobility, and compassion, she comes to the fore in the second half of the *novela* and is a driving force toward the conclusion.

300 Scudieri Ruggieri, José. "Notas a la *Arcadia*, de Lope de Vega." *CHA*, nos. 161-62 (May-June 1963), pp. 577-605.
The women in Lope's *Arcadia* are more human than in other pastoral novels because they incorporate real women in the life of the dramatist, with their real emotions and rivalries.

301 Serralta, Frédéric. *La Renegada de Valladolid: Trayectoria dramática de un tema popular*. Toulouse: Institut d'Études Hispaniques, 1970.
The theme of the Renegada de Valladolid, very popular throughout the Golden Age, first appears in a sixteenth-century *canción de ciegos*, in which the intent is clearly to reinforce the faith. The theme evolves in the theater, gradually disintegrating, in three main phases: religious, secular, and burlesque. Pedro Herrero's *La Cautiva de Valladolid* shows some slight modifications of the original version, adding, for example, an account of the protagonist's love. In Lorenzo de Avellaneda's *La vida, conversión y muerte de Agueda de Acevedo, dama de Valladolid*, the protagonist is not yet the energetic and passionate woman of later plays, but neither is she a puppet whose decisions are

explained simply by the weight of tradition. In the quite secular auto, La Cautiva de Valladolid, Agueda is no longer a passive victim of men or of the demon. She displays traits which later become characteristic: constancy and strength of will. La Renegada de Valladolid by Belmonte, Moreto, and Martínez Meneses presents a heroine, now named Isabel, who is neither victim nor instrument but a firm, rebellious, and passionate woman. Her strong personality, which succumbs only to the blows of a superior fatality, gives her, at times, the dimensions of a romantic heroine. In La Renegada de Valladolid by Monteser, Solís, and Silva, a burlesque comedy, the character Agueda reveals parodical exaggeration. It is not only her energy which is emphasized, but also her insolence. Her reactions are often those of a virago. Diego Granados y Mosquera's mojiganga La Renegada de Valladolid completely deflates the protagonist, leaving her without nobility.

302 Serrano García, Virtudes. "La función de la mujer en la estructura de tres dramas de honor del siglo XVII." Estudios literarios dedicados al profesor Mariano Baquero Goyanes. Edited by V. Polo García. Murcia: Nogués, 1974, pp. 495-510.

In Spanish Golden Age theater it is hard to find heroines with a distinctive personality. The lack of interest in feminine characters, particularly in dramas of honor, evolves gradually, however, toward a more positive valuation. Near the end of the Baroque period, Rojas Zorrilla elevates woman to the category of active heroine.

Serrano García compares the heroines of three honor plays, Lope's La desdichada Estefanía, Calderón's A secreto agravio secreta venganza, and Rojas's Casarse por vengarse. Whereas Lope and Calderón give their women a schematic characterization and marginal role, Rojas makes his heroine vigorous and capable of deciding her own fate against the judgment of her husband. Blanca, who takes on the courage and firmness traditionally reserved for men, becomes the true protagonist of the play.

303 Serrano Poncela, Segundo. "Aldonza la andaluza lozana en Roma." CA, 21 (May-June 1962), 117-32.

Delicado's Aldonza, an original creation closer to reality than to fiction, possesses a complexity unknown in other heroines of novelesque or picaresque plots. She is a feminine type without antecedents in Spanish literature and without imitations in the Golden Age.

304 Shepard, Sanford. "Prostitutes and Picaros in Inquisitional Spain." Neohelicon, 3, nos. 1-2 (1975), 365-72.

The Biblical figure which compares the faithless of Israel to the harlot or adulteress, becomes a metaphor in the Spanish picaresque novels of the Inquisitional period. The protagonists of such works as Delicado's *La Lozana andaluza*, López de Ubeda's *La pícara Justina*, and Salas Barbadillo's *La hija de Celestina* are *conversas* and prostitutes. The real historical situation, in which women of Jewish background were often forced to choose between prostitution and starvation, probably gave immediacy to the Biblical allegory.

305 Shervill, R. N. "Lope's Ways with Women." *BCom*, 15 (Fall 1963), 10-13.

Whereas the heroines of Lope's secular *comedias* are essentially idealized beings whose purity seems modeled on that of the Virgin Mary, his Old Testament and non-Spanish heroines personify some of the baser qualities of womanhood, in accord with the medieval view of Eve. Shervill discusses specifically five Old Testament plays with their respective feminine protagonists, each of whom is quite freely treated by the dramatist. Even Esther of *La hermosa Ester*, who more closely approximates the conventional Spanish heroine, is depicted as possessing so much guile as to become something of a *femme fatale*.

306 Sims, Edna N. *El antifeminismo en la literatura española hasta 1560*. Dissertation. Washington, D. C.: Catholic University of America, 1970. See Chs. IV and V. Also Bogotá: Editorial Andes, 1973.

Chapter IV deals with Delicado's *La lozana andaluza* and the anonymous *Lazarillo de Tormes*; Chapter V, with the humanists Juan Luis Vives, Cristóbal de Villalón, and Luis de León. Delicado portrays Lozana as ridiculous and hypocritical, indeed, as the worst woman of her period. He also presents other negative feminine types, whose most evident vices, apart from prostitution, are greed, superstition, and vanity. The antifeminism of *Lazarillo de Tormes* is manifested through the ignoble attitude and unscrupulous acts which the various women, including his mother, unknowingly teach the impressionable Lazarillo.

The humanists, while continuing to enumerate feminine vices, also draw from Christian and pagan concepts, elements of a recipe for the ideal woman. On the one hand, they envision a woman who strives for the harmonious development of all her faculties, enjoyment of this life, and complete equality with man. On the other hand, they propose an exemplary woman who, while aspiring to the primitive simplicity of the Gospels, is a fundamentally weak woman who can only be saved if she seeks interior religiosity.

307 _____. "Notes on the Negative Image of Woman in Spanish Literature." CLA Journal, 19 (June 1976), 468-83.

In the early picaresque novel there is an accelerated projection of the vices previously described as characterizing women. Now the impulse which marks the comportment of woman is attributed to the unhappy economic situation to which she finds herself almost permanently condemned.

The humanist writers who come afterward continue to present feminine vices, but they make an honest effort to be objective. They are primarily interested in the betterment of society, and their understanding of the important role of woman in this mission inspires them to instruct her.

308 Sletsjöe, Leif. "Sobre el tópico de los ojos verdes." Strenae: Estudios de filología e historia dedicados al Profesor Manuel García Blanco. Salamanca: Universidad de Salamanca, 1962, pp. 445-59.

The topos of green eyes, developed in the Middle Ages, has two basic currents, one negative and derogatory; one, completely positive. Cervantes, Lope, and Quevedo are among Spanish writers of the Golden Age who use the motif with positive connotations. Tirso's preference for black eyes is an exception. Green eyes, which are linked with fair hair and skin, are not only an element of ideal feminine beauty, but are also indicative of aristocratic birth, perhaps suggesting that the woman is an Old Christian.

309 Sloman, Albert E. "Lope's El mejor alcalde el rey: Addendum to a Note by Sturgis E. Leavitt." BCom, 7 (Fall 1955), 17-19.

Feliciana is an important character in the play, above all, because she is a foil to Tello, with whom she is inevitably associated. Their portrayal in Act I as having much in common accentuates the differences which emerge in Act II. Feliciana's pity sets in relief Tello's brutality and ruthlessness; her prudence, his lack of the same virtue. These are the qualities for which she is ultimately rewarded.

310 _____. "The Structure of Calderón's La vida es sueño." MLR, 48 (July 1953), 293-300.

Rosaura is both the means and the proof of Segismundo's conversion.

311 Smith, John D. "Metaphysical Descriptions of Women in the First Sonnets of Góngora." Hispania, 56 (April 1973), 244-48.

In the sonnets written between 1582 and 1585 a certain pattern can be perceived in Góngora's descriptions of women.

Smith discusses several individual sonnets, including one in which the lady is a sacred temple, a structure of divine origin. The portrait we can construct of her--white complexion, small red mouth, green eyes, blonde hair--is created entirely through metaphors. In another example, the lady has leonine characteristics and is able to dominate the strongest of men.

312 Snow, Joseph. "La Tragicomedia de Calisto y Melibea de Juan de Sedeño: Algunas observaciones a su primera escena comparada con la original." Celestinesca, 2, no. 2 (1978), 13-27.

Sedeño's Melibea of the first scene is more communicative than that of Rojas. She defines herself more clearly because she says more. One cannot accuse her of being overly cautious, timid, or uncertain of the meaning of Calisto's words. She is not overwhelmed by the fervor of his declarations but knows how to respond. More rational, self-possessed, and self-confident than the original, she is a determined woman in whom there is no room for coquetry. She expresses herself more directly, and her disdain for Calisto is stronger and more personal.

313 Sola-Solé, Josep M. "Sobre el tema de 'la mujer hermosa'." Studies in Honor of Tatiana Fotitch. Edited by J. M. Sola-Solé et al. Washington, D. C.: Catholic University of America Press and Consortium Press, 1972, pp. 303-14.

The old theme of la mujer hermosa, according to which a woman's beauty is detrimental for the woman herself and dangerous for the social order surrounding her, appears in such Golden Age works and writers as Luis de León's La perfecta casada, Baltasar Gracián's El criticón, Quevedo, and the comedia. La Estrella de Sevilla can be considered the maximum exponent of the theme. The idea that only the woman of noble origin is capable of escaping the misfortune and danger inherent to feminine beauty, is a variation which occurs in such works as Cervantes's La ilustre fregona and La gitanilla, and Juan Pérez de Montalbán's La desgraciada amistad. In the Baroque period especially, feminine beauty is felt to be, within the general framework of human vanity and the futility of life, something perishable and illusory.

314 Solé-Leris, A. "Psychological Realism in the Pastoral Novel: Gil Polo's Diana enamorada." BHS, 39 (January 1962), 43-47.

Gil Polo shows how Felicia, applying human wisdom rather than magic art, brings about the reconciliation of the lovers by natural persuasion and careful psychological preparation. She bases her action and argument on her knowledge of the human heart, and on the shrewd assessment of the characters' states of mind and probable reactions.

315 Soons, Alan. *Alonso de Castillo Solórzano*. Boston: Twayne, 1978. See Ch. 4.

In this chapter, Soons comments on Castillo's feminine swindlers, who are not so attractive as their male counterparts. One reason is that the *pícaro* is intelligent, while the *buscona* is simply astute. The *buscona* is barely present in *Lazarillo*, dominates certain chapters of Alemán's *Guzmán de Alfarache*, and later takes over entire works, the most striking example being Salas Barbadillo's *La ingeniosa Elena, hija de Celestina*. In this prostitute's biography, Salas prunes away the misogynistic platitudes of former writers and allows Elena to reflect on her actions and upbringing. There is no special knowledge of the feminine soul, however; Salas's voice consistently echoes the voice of the social order. We can conclude that some writers chose a female criminal as their subject because of its sensationalism.

316 Sorensen, Jorge E. "*La mejor espigadera*: Una glosa dramática del Libro de Rut." *RF*, 90 (1978), 70-77.

In the first two acts of this Tirsean play, Ruth is a proud woman who uses others to achieve her worldly goals. She is motivated, not by the consciousness of her mission according to the prophecy, but by the glory which can accrue to her as a result of it. From the beginning of the third act, she displays a notable change, the result of a profound *desengaño*. She is now the Ruth of the Bible.

317 Spieker, Joseph B. "El feminismo como clave estructural en las *novelle* de doña María de Zayas." *ExTL*, 6, no. 2 (1978), 153-60.

Zayas's general aim, that women be warned of men's deceits, appears to be a rebuttal of the notion expressed in the subtitle of the medieval *Sendebar*: "el libro de los engaños e asayamientos de las mujeres." Zayas seeks to demonstrate woman's competence, champion her equality with man, and defend her against false and unjust criticism. Her protagonists stand out as constant, competent women who know how to avenge themselves against an offender. In the majority of her *novelas*, these brave and virtuous heroines contrast diametrically with their vile and reprehensible masculine counterparts.

318 Spitzer, Leo. "The Figure of Fénix in Calderón's *El príncipe constante*." *Critical Essays*, pp. 137-60.

In his discussion of Fénix's character, Spitzer observes

that she is basically selfish. Beautiful and beauty-seeking, she is capable of acting or reacting only from an esthetic stance. In the end, she is pushed around like a piece on a chessboard, fittingly enough, since she, who could not love, has no right to a will of her own or to a real life.

319 _____. "Lope de Vega's 'Al triunfo de Judit' (Rimas humanas LXXVIII)." MLN, 69 (January 1954), 1-11.
Lope's heroine is a Judith triumphans, an ancient imperator as well as a warrior of God. With the word casta, Lope has chosen to maintain the orthodox simplistic psychology of the Biblical account, according to which the pious Judith was capable of her great act because of the chaste life she had led during her widowhood. Lope suggests that she could be attractive but not attracted.

320 Stanton, Edward F. "Cervantes and Cinthio: An Episode in Persiles y Sigismunda." Hispano-Italic Studies, no. 1 (1976), pp. 32-38.
Doña Guiomar's story is a kind of microcosm of the whole novel; she personifies the Christian virtue sought and attained by Persiles and Sigismunda. Whereas Cinthio's Livia is a somewhat abstract and impersonal type, Cervantes's Guiomar is a true character, who, nevertheless, represents certain moral qualities.

321 Stroud, Matthew D. "Social-Comic Anagnorisis in La dama duende." BCom, 29 (Fall 1977), 96-102.
Angela, the protagonist and prime mover of the action in this play by Calderón, is a victimized woman. She illustrates the plight of the woman who, constrained by a rigid society, is forced to use deceit in order to make any sort of self-assertive overtures to the man of her desires. Only by denying her own identity is she ultimately accepted back into the society which does not appreciate her as a clever individual intellect, but simply as a sex object or docile wife.

322 Sturm, Sara H., and Harlan G. Sturm. "The Astronomical Metaphor in La Estrella de Sevilla." Hispania, 52 (May 1969), 193-97.
Estrella not only embodies the ideal of purity and nobility which the king first attempts to corrupt but later respects; she is also, in conjunction with Busto, a representation of the divine guidance which the king first tries to ignore but finally accepts.

323 Sylvania, Lena Evelyn V. Doña María de Zayas y Sotomayor: A Contribution to the Study of Her Works. 1922; rpt. New

York: AMS Press, 1966. See pp. 7-17. Also in RR, 13 (July-September 1922), 197-213; 14 (January-March 1923), 199-232.

Zayas presents woman's love as so great and unselfish that it stands all tests. In her zeal to portray a loving, trusting martyr, she sometimes falls into the error of creating a simpleton whose blindness is completely ridiculous. Yet, in El prevenido engañado, she argues in favor of the intelligent woman, wise to the ways of the world, as opposed to the stupid, ignorant fool, incapable of a deep or sustained sentiment or of preserving her honor.

324 Templin, E. H. "The Mother in the Comedia of Lope de Vega." HR, 3 (July 1935), 219-44.

The mother in Tirso de Molina, Guillén de Castro, and Lope de Vega is both numerically and dramatically important; and some mothers of significance are found in Mira de Amescua, Pérez de Montalbán, and Vélez de Guevara. Most belong to the upper middle stratum, the nobility, or royalty, are definitely maternal in their attitude toward their children, are highly virtuous, and are the object of some form of persecution or injustice. Nearly all are preeminently creatures of emotion. Approximately one third of the more important figures are unmarried mothers. Lope's and Tirso's figures differ in that the former stresses both paciencia and valor, while Tirso is a decided partisan of the latter virtue. In general, the type is an ideal fusion of traits absorbed from Spanish society with those of literary prototypes.

325 Testas, Jean. "Le féminisme de Francisco de Rojas Zorrilla." Mélanges offerts à Charles Vincent Aubrun. Vol. 2. Paris: Editions Hispaniques, 1975, pp. 303-22.

Of the comediantes, Rojas Zorrilla offers the most remarkable feminine characters. Plays such as Entre bobos anda el juego, Progne y Filomena, Del rey abajo, ninguno, La vida en el ataúd, and Cada cual lo que le toca, offer good examples of heroines presented by an admiring and understanding writer. One way in which Rojas differs from other dramatists of the period is in his delicate analysis of the development of feminine desire as an interior event, rather than the stark presentation of conquest and its aftermath. His heroines have both a sense of their own rights with regard to love, rights they declare openly, and a sense of their own responsibility for their choices. Indeed, Rojas, whose feminism is the fruit of a broad humanism which questions social values, presents not only female but also male characters who reflect and choose, instead of blindly following social laws, and who submit to no other absolute idealogy than that of love.

326 Thompson, Jennifer. "The Structure of Cervantes' Las dos doncellas." BHS, 40 (July 1963), 144-50.

In the case of Teodosia and Leocadia, there is not an unnecessary duplication of roles. Each is essential because her story constitutes one aspect of certain cuestiones de amor, around which the novela is constructed. The deliberate similarities between the two women underline the importance of such issues as which is the more unhappy; which has the greater claim, legally and emotionally, on Marco Antonio; and which has the greater cause for jealousy.

*327 Torres, Federico. Dulcinea del Toboso. Barcelona: Editorial Selección, 1955.

328 Torres Delgado, René. "Fabia, hija de Celestina y nieta de Trotaconventos." Atenea, Puerto Rico, 9 (1973), 131-38.

Fabia of Lope's El caballero de Olmedo is a go-between, sagacious observer, master of the science of the human heart, feigned peddler of trifles, eloquent rhetorician, Epicurean disciple of Bacchus and Venus, inventor of intrigue, repairer of maidenheads, and conjurer of demons. Like her predecessors Trotaconventos and Celestina, she acts as a deus ex machina in the tragedy of the lovers who entrust themselves to her.

329 Trachman, Sadie Edith. Cervantes' Women of Literary Tradition. New York: Inst. de las Españas en los EEUU, 1932.

Although Cervantes takes a few advanced or unique stands regarding woman, such as advocacy of a young woman's right to choose her own husband, justification of woman's passional errors, and opposition to punishment by death whether a woman be guilty or not of infidelity; his conception of woman in general is nevertheless quite conventional. Likewise, a vast number of his feminine characters owe their creation entirely or in part to diverse literary sources, which he transforms to a greater or lesser degree, often with features taken from real life. These feminine types in Cervantes are the Mooress, subgroups of which include the convert, the lover of valor, the lover of her Christian slave, and the sorceress; the female Christian slave; the pastoral heroine, which embraces the purely conventional shepherdess, the adopter of the pastoral life, the fickle shepherdess, the egotistic one, and the scorner of love; the type which inspires chivalry, including the idealized woman, the wrongfully accused one, and the woman carried off and rescued; the knightly type; the courageous lover; the Dido type; the mythological type; the Italian and Spanish novelesque type, including the vengeful woman, the defender of her own chastity, the temporarily dishonored woman, the clandestine spouse, the faithless spouse, the vile defrauder, and the unchaste servant; the Celestina type; the coquette; the staunch performer of a promise; the sagacious type; the innocent, unsophisticated type; the constant lover; the girl unblemished by her milieu; and the wandering princess.

330 Trinker, Martha K. de. *Las mujeres en el Don Quijote de Cervantes comparadas con las mujeres en los dramas de Shakespeare*. México: Talls. de la Editorial Cultura, 1938.

Women play a relatively small role in the vast world of Cervantes's creations. There are two basic groups of feminine figures in the *Quixote*: realistic types, excellent portraits taken from the humble class, of whom Teresa Panza is the most lovable and the best drawn, and literary types informed by the author's own ideals. Cervantes treats his realistic feminine characters with smiling generosity and understanding. In his handling of the others he manifests the same ideal as that formulated in Luis de León's *La perfecta casada*.

Cervantes does not understand woman completely and never really rises above the general opinion of the period that she is an imperfect animal. Marcela is the exception that proves the rule. The novelist does not regard woman as evil, simply as weak and needing man's help in order to maintain her virtue.

331 Trueblood, Alan S. *Experience and Artistic Expression in Lope de Vega: The Making of La Dorotea*. Cambridge: Harvard University Press, 1974. See especially Sec. XII.

Because Lope gathers up in Dorotea reminiscences of several women in his emotional life and associations with others of literary extraction, she embodies, more than any other figure in his production, the eternal feminine, which never ceased to attract him as the quintessence of the world's appeal. She is also woman as muse, the object of the poet's cult. Dorotea's voice is at times Lope's own, especially in the expression of *desengaño*.

Gerarda is endowed to the highest degree with Lope's sense of immersion in life as a game and, at the same time, of ultimate detachment from it. Her playfulness erases all traces of viciousness from her nature and converts her procuring from a profession into an engaging pastime; Gerarda becomes an entertainer. In the last analysis she chooses life in preference to profit. Her ultimate disinterestedness serves as a sign that she is closer to her creator than to her literary prototype, Celestina.

332 _____. "Masters and Servants: La Dorotea vis-à-vis the Comedia." KRQ, 16 (1969), 55-61.
The maidservants in Lope's La Dorotea show more familiarity with their mistresses than do those of the comedia, as they are, in fact, close companions and near equals. Dorotea's two servants, Celia and Felipa, though struck from the same mold, display different personalities and play different roles. Celia's function is to express the voice that Dorotea is suppressing, to bring out the full sweep of her confused and tormented state of mind. Felipa is Dorotea's surrogate.

333 Tyler, R. W. "Algunas versiones de la leyenda de la 'Reina Sevilla' en la primera mitad del Siglo de Oro." Actas del Segundo Congreso Internacional de Hispanistas. Edited by J. Sánchez Romeralo and N. Poulussen. Nijmegen, Netherlands: Janssen Brothers Ltd., 1967, pp. 635-41.
The author mentions various works which employ the motif of the Reina Sevilla, the name given to the legend of a woman falsely accused of infidelity but finally vindicated.

334 _____. "False Accusation of Women in 'Plays Probably by Lope' de Vega." BCom, 17 (Fall 1965), 13-15.
Tyler discusses briefly seven plays in which an unsuccessful suitor or other interested party falsely accuses a woman of adultery or a similar crime.

335 _____. "False Accusations of Women in the Plays of Tirso de Molina." KRQ, 16 (1969), 119-23.
Apart from Lope, Tirso seems to have used the motif of the false accusation of infidelity or adultery on the part of a woman more than any other Golden Age dramatist. However, Tirso's false accusations lack the variety and development of Lope's.

336 Ullman, Pierre L. "The Surrogates of Baroque Marcela and Mannerist Leandra." Revista de Estudios Hispánicos, 5 (October 1971), 307-19.
Cervantes's Marcela and Leandra each obtain a drove of admirers who behave in the same way, bringing about similar situations, yet the two heroines are totally different. The first left home alone and, though surrounded by men, appears devoid of interest in the opposite sex, being primarily concerned to maintain her freedom and honor. The second left home with a man and as a result has lost freedom, honor, and the company of men. Marcela is the flesh and blood virgin of a secularized religious tale. Rocinante, in the incident with the unwilling mares, becomes her ironic

surrogate. Leandra, a dubious figure, has skewed symbols and a split surrogation: the image of the Virgin carried in religious procession and the wayward goat Manchada.

337 Valbuena Prat, Angel. "Isabel Freyre en las 'Eglogas' de Garcilaso." HAG, 2, 483-93.
In the "Egloga III" Garcilaso associates Elisa (Isabel) with Inés de Castro in the figure of the nymph Nise, thus mythifying his beloved.

338 Van Beysterveldt, Antony. "La inversión del amor cortés en Moreto." CHA, no. 283 (January 1974), pp. 88-114.
From the Eglogas of Juan del Encina to the seventeenth-century comedias, the phenomenon of disdain is a constant in the psychology of the dama confronted by the male's amorous insistence. This disdain is one aspect of a behavioral system proper to the ideal of courtly love typical of fifteenth-century Spanish love poetry. Of the two divergent paths taken by courtly love, the ascetic-Christian and the Neoplatonic-Christian, the two springing from diametrically opposite conceptions of woman, only the first finds a place in Golden Age theater. According to this current, woman is a temptation of the devil, an instrument of pleasure with which man is animalized. The comedia does not lack protests against this attitude. The resistance to men by the female protagonists in Lope's Los milagros del desprecio and La venganza de las mujeres seems to be based on their loftier concept of woman and indignation at the humiliating role imposed upon her.
From the point of view of social class, there are two basic explanations for the phenomenon of disdain as it is manifested in the comedia. In its direct relationship to the attitude of "cruelty" and "ingratitude" proper to the dama of courtly poetry, it is a sign of gentle upbringing, something which sets the noble woman apart from the lower class. For the plebs, represented in the comedia chiefly by the servants, this disdain is a typical expression of the resistance which woman opposes to the aggressive sexual instinct of man. The confrontation between master and servant, with their different attitudes toward life, woman, and love, is an almost obligatory element in every comedia. The servant normally succeeds in imposing on his master his more realistic or cynical ideas, such as that a woman's disdain can be conquered by matching disdain on the part of the man, because the woman needs him as much as or more than he desires her.
In Moreto's play the inversion of courtly love is manifested in Diana herself, as well as in other characters.

Her response of disdain is based, in the last analysis, on a rational rejection of courtly love. Nevertheless, it is clear that she is not opposed to love as such. The definition of love she proposes to Carlos, a union or fusion of two souls, is an ideal very rarely found in lyric poetry of the fifteen century and only fully affirmed in mystical poetry of the sixteenth century.

339 Van Praag, J. A. "La pícara en la literatura española." The Spanish Review, 3 (November 1936), 63-74.

With López de Ubeda's La pícara Justina, woman enters the picaresque novel as protagonist. The pícara does not supplant the pícaro but is equally if not more successful with the public. Qualities or conditions shared by the pícaro and pícara are their low extraction, their membership in a non-Arian race, and their poverty, but the females seem to overcome economic difficulties more readily, hunger not being so important in their lives as in those of their male counterparts. Both are astute, calculating, and untroubled by scruples, compassion, or love, yet the pícara especially conquers us by her charm. Both are motivated by greed, which for the pícara entails pursuit of a rich, preferably old, husband. The pícara even more than the pícaro knows the importance of a good reputation; her language and the tone of her conversation are those of a woman of good breeding. She is usually intellectually superior to the men she encounters, and she has at her disposal, besides her innate astuteness, corporal beauty, which she knows how to take advantage of. She generally commits no crimes except to trick the unwary; she is not a prostitute or procuress, though it is possible that on growing old she will become such. The pícara always moves in a social milieu superior to that of the pícaro.

Although it is clear that the pícara has the sympathy of her creator, the works in which she appears manifest an antifeminist or quasi-antifeminist character; in all of them we find Sempronio's diatribe against women in one form or other.

The average dama of the Spanish comedia, though of a different social class from the pícara and lacking her freedom of movement, is essentially similar in her character and way of thinking.

340 _____. "Sobre las novelas de María de Zayas." Clavileño, 3, no. 15 (1952), 42-43.

One deduces from Zayas's novelas that husbands, often disaffected, went so far as to maltreat their wives. This is surprising because the comedia and novela of the period usually give the impression that the man always looked after and protected, not only his own wife, daughter, or other female relative, but any woman.

341 Vasileski, Irma V. María de Zayas y Sotomayor: Su época y su obra. Madrid: Plaza Mayor, 1973.
Zayas presents various feminine types, including the idealized woman of conservative circles, the woman of the world, and the woman whose psychological qualities border on the pathological. In none of her twenty novelas is there a heroine with a genuine religious vocation; all have first chosen another kind of love and suffered great disillusionment from it. In women of the upper classes, love is idealistic and disinterested; in those of the lower class, it is the obsessive desire for a lover or husband.
In general, Zayas confronts woman's idealism with the cynical egotism of man, the deceived woman being presented as superior to her burlador. Although Zayas complains of the position to which women have been relegated by men, and although the naturally varonil type does not appear in her works, many of her feminine characters display masculine strength and conduct when deprived by circumstances of the protection of father and brother, and when love or honor spurs them on.

342 Venegas, José. Dulcinea y Sancho. Buenos Aires: Editorial Centro Republicano Español, 1949. See especially pp. 29-64.
Dulcinea is the chimerical archetype of the dreamed-of woman Cervantes never knew. Born as a subproduct of Don Quixote's madness, she soon becomes the madness itself. Cervantes caricatures Dulcinea through Aldonza, providing a violent contrast to the limitless exaltations of Don Quixote, but he does not intend thereby to convince us that the perfections which fantasy attributes to the beloved woman are in reality only the repulsive coarseness of an Aldonza. What matters is to have Dulcinea in the heart, whatever be her real image.

343 Veras D'Ocón, Ernesto. "Los retratos de Dulcinea y Maritornes." ACer, 1 (1951), 249-71.
The protrait of Dulcinea represents the superación and ironización of the medieval rhetorical protrait of the lady, while that of Maritornes represents the mythification of the infrahuman. They are equally distant from reality but with opposite signs.

344 Viedma, Cristina. "Del misterio de Marcela, ingenua y mujer fatal." EstLit, no. 383 (November 18, 1967), p. 14.
There is a radical ambivalence about Cervantes's Marcela, a girl of simple tastes, candid and pure, with something of

the mystic about her. She is, however, also a mujer fatal, an angel of death. Free in one sense, because she has overcome the slavery of social compromises, she is yet the prisoner of her own fatal beauty. Marcela represents the ancient and essential conflict of the human condition; she is a victim of the world, and in turn, the world is her victim.

345 Viera, David J. "Actitudes hacia la educación de la mujer en las letras clásicas hispánicas." Thesaurus, 31 (Jaunary-April 1976), 160-64.

Many Spanish Renaissance didactic moral writers and, to a certain extent, some mystics, such as Teresa of Avila, thought that wisdom acquired by study and intellectual debate was not appropriate to women, and that her participation in the same would result in error, confusion, and moral degeneration. This opinion coexisted with the more liberal posture supported by writers like Juan Luis Vives, Antonio de Guevara, and Cristóbal de Villalón. Guevara insisted on wisdom more than any other virtue in his blueprint for the ideal woman. Nevertheless, even those who approved of the learned woman did not accept her presence in many disciplines, especially theology.

346 _____. "'El hombre cuerdo no debe fiar de la mujer ningún secreto', como tema de la literatura clásica hispánica." Thesaurus, 30 (September-December 1975), 557-60.

Two texts in which the title theme appears are Antonio de Guevara's "Epístola 37" and Cristóbal de Villalón's Scholastico.

347 Vollmer, Sylvia M. "The Position of Woman in Spain as Seen in Spanish Literature." Hispania, 8 (October 1925), 211-36; (November 1925), 303-48.

Luis de León's La perfecta casada suggests that knowledge in women is at variance with happiness. There is no hint that the author had any conception of woman as the equal of man or that she should be allowed any social or moral freedom as an independent soul. Cervantes, more than any other Golden Age writer, gives a true picture of Spanish ideals and customs regarding women. However, it is Lope de Vega who depicts woman with the greatest tenderness and who best portrays her valor and spirit of sacrifice in the most difficult situations. Tirso de Molina draws women out of their conventional setting and endows them with a freedom of action which was impossible in real life. In Alarcón's Las paredes oyen, a woman takes it upon herself to punish slander. Her action is unusual but plausible because she is a widow. Calderón's *El alcalde de Zalamea* shows a considerable advance in the male attitude toward honor and women. In this play, the innocent woman is not made to pay for the outrage done through her to the family honor; rather, vengeance is taken on the perpetrator of the crime.

348 Vosters, Simon A. "Lope de Vega y las damas doctas." *Actas del Tercer Congreso*, pp. 909-21.

In the argument over the intellectual ability of women, Lope is unconditionally on the side of the panegyrists. On the occasion of St. Teresa's beatification, Lope also honored the Barcelonese woman Juliana Morell, zealously defending, in the process, woman's capacity for learning and even attacking some misogynistic passages of the Bible, "mal citados y peor interpretados." Among the numerous texts in which Lope honors cultured women is Book IV of *Peregrino en su patria*, in which he claims that many contemporary Spanish women are superior to famous *savantes* of ancient Greece and Rome. If it is true that Lope's *Laurel de Apolo* includes some very secondary female writers, partly out of generosity, partly in return for their admiration of him, it is also true that Lope is the only person who gives us any details on the life and works of many otherwise unknown women authors, who helped define the literary environment of the time, if not by their talent, by their musical gifts, enthusiasm, and support.

349 _____. "Lope de Vega y Juan Ravisio Téxtor: Nuevos datos." *Ibero*, Nueva época, 2 (1975), 69-103.

Lope makes extensive use of Jean Tixier de Ravisy's *Officina* in the catalogues of learned and illustrious women which he inserts in many of his dramatic and nondramatic works. His lists include sixty-four women who can be considered *doctas*, thirty-three of them from Antiquity and thirty-one from the Renaissance.

Vosters also mentions several earlier Spanish panegyrists of learned women, some of whose eulogies acquire a hagiographical character.

350 Wade, Gerald E. "The Anonymous *La reina penitente*." *BCom*, 7 (Spring 1955), 3-8.

Although England is the setting for this play which incorporates the Potiphar's wife theme, there is no similarity between the character Isabel and the historical Queen Elizabeth, except in name.

351 _____. "La comicidad de *Don Gil de las calzas verdes* de Tirso de Molina." *Revista de Archivos, Bibliotecas y Museos*, 76 (1973), 475-86.

Among the comic devices employed in this play is the degradación of values accepted by Tirso's society, such as insistence on the domination of man and the submission of woman. It is obvious that, without being conscious of it in our contemporary terms, Tirso was a precursor of women's liberation. His female characters usually prove stronger than the men, as in this play. The belittling of male and certain female values is also clear in the scene in which Juana, disguised as a man, wins the love of two women. Other feminine values which suffer comic degradation are rivalry for the same man and thirst for money.

352 Waley, Pamela. "Garcilaso, Isabel and Elena: The Growth of a Legend." BHS, 56 (January 1979), 11-15.
It is not necessarily true that Garcilaso wrote no poetry to his wife, Elena de Zúñiga. Sonnets IV, V, VIII, and IX may very possibly be dedicated to her. Only three poems can incontrovertibly be held to concern Isabel Freire: the copla "Aviéndose casado su dama" and the first and third eclogues.

353 Wardropper, Bruce W. "El burlador de Sevilla: A Tragedy of Errors." Philological Quarterly, 36 (January 1957), 61-71.
The women in this Tirsean play are as much victims of self-deception as of don Juan's deceits. The theme of women who, in their trust of men, are naïve and prone to disillusionment, is announced from the beginning. Among the objects of don Juan's attention is doña Ana, the only realistic female, who neither mistakes the intruder's identity nor falls prey to his flattery. She and her father are the only ones to triumph over don Juan, just as in Calderón's La vida es sueño, Rosaura and Clotaldo are the only characters consistently faithful to unselfish principles.

354 _____. "The Diana of Montemayor: Revaluation and Interpretation." SPh, 48 (1951), 126-44.
In the age-old controversy over the nature of women, Montemayor, on the whole, sides with their admirers. He does, however, recognize that women have defects, the major one being inconstancy. Like his hero, Sireno, Montemayor oscillates between the two traditional views, an attitude which is psychologically more truthful than the extremes of praise and sarcasm.
The pastoral setting of the novel grants women an equality with men denied them by the social conventions of an urban milieu. The author not only recognizes that the feminine point of view is different; he gives it its fullest expression in the Spanish Renaissance. For the first time men were able to see themselves as women saw them.

Wardropper

355 _____. "Lope's La dama boba and Baroque Comedy." BCom, 13 (Fall 1961), 1-3.

The unmarried heroine of a Golden Age comedy is an idle chatterbox; her life, a shallow stream of lovemaking in conventional social situations. The wife of the more tragic honor plays, on the contrary, is a woman whose life runs deep, sanctified by a conjugal love made firm by her constant preoccupation with the honor of her husband. Nevertheless, the female character in comedy is becoming, moving toward the essential reality which is the assumption of a husband's flesh and honor in marriage.

Thus Finea of La dama boba is transformed through love's teaching into the potential wife of a serious honor play. As a result, she may expect to progress from the world of appearances to that of reality, from becoming to being.

356 _____. "'La más bella niña'." SPh, 63 (1966), 661-76.

In contrast to the vagueness regarding the relations between the girl and the man who has just gone off to war, is the precision with which the girl analyzes her feelings. Not satisfied with the passive role of the mother as confidante, as found in the traditional Frauenlied, Góngora imagines a kind of moral struggle between the complaining girl and the listening mother. After she has quarrelled with her mother, imputing to her the responsibility for the amorous crisis, the girl moderates her antagonism a little and exhorts her mother to share her suffering. In the end, however, the girl recognizes that she must bear her anguish alone, must be sufficient unto herself, rather than depend on maternal sympathy.

357 _____. "La novela como retrato: El arte de Francisco Delicado." NRFH, 7, nos. 3-4 (1953), 475-88.

Delicado strives to explain Lozana's actions in terms of both her psyche and her milieu. She is a feminine version of Cellini, a creature of nature, dynamic and without scruples. She desires independence above all else, and to this end she directs all her talents, chief of which is her don de gentes. Lozana is also the quasi-allegorical nucleus of the Roma meretrice.

358 _____. "The Reluctant Novice: A Critical Approach to Spanish Traditional Song." RR, 55 (December 1964), 241-47.

Wardropper discusses a villancico, first printed by the sixteenth-century musicologist Francisco de Salinas, in the light of traditional motifs. Explicitly, we have the conflict between two generations which love and respect one another but which fail miserably to understand one another.

The older woman is primarily concerned with the problem of honor, which can be satisfactorily solved on the social level by flight to the convent. The young girl experiences a vital urge and the terror of its frustration, coupled with a profound contempt for society's qué dirán. The emotions aroused in the girl and her mother have been deliberately suppressed, but the pathos of the situation is effectively conveyed.

359 Weiner, Jack. "Cristina de Suecia en dos obras de Calderón de la Barca." BCom, 31 (Spring 1979), 25-31.
Weiner discusses the comedia Afectos de odio y amor and the auto sacramental La protestación de la fe. In the first work, the dramatist describes Cristerna, or Cristina, as a great sovereign who knows how to protect her country and in whom beauty and intelligence are united to soldierly courage, traits which recall other Calderonian heroines. Cristerna is a feminist who defends the right of women to govern. She is also a great huntswoman, a description perhaps inspired by a portrait of her done by the French painter Sébastien Bourdon. In the auto, Cristina is the force which at first keeps northern Europe outside the Catholic orbit and then becomes the only hope for converting Sweden to Catholicism.

360 _____. "Lázaro y las mujeres: Protagonistas que comparten un sino parecido." Palabra y Hombre, Xalapa, México, no. 47 (1968), pp. 359-65.
The author of Lazarillo belongs to the pro-feminist rather than the misogynous tradition. Always in evidence is the thesis that women are consistently treated by men as their inferiors; that women suffer more than men and are more often victims. They are unable to rise out of this condition because they take it for granted. Yet, as a general rule, the women whom Lazarillo encounters are superior to the men in human qualities such as kindness and charity.

361 _____. "Una posible razón de Urraca para matar a su hermano Sancho: Una contribución de Guillén de Castro al Tema Cidiano." Revue des Langues Romanes, 79 (1969), 173-95.
The enmity and rivalry between Urraca and Sancho for Rodrigo's affection is a possible original contribution by Castro to the Cid theme. Jealousy induces Urraca to kill Sancho, who could separate her permanently from Rodrigo. On the other hand, she never displays envy or jealousy toward Ximena, whom she does not consider a significant rival.

362 Welles, Marcia L. "María de Zayas y Sotomayor and Her novela cortesana: A Re-evaluation." BHS, 55 (October 1978), 301-10.

Beyond the explicit intent to depict the basic Hero-Villain struggle between Woman and Man, there is, in Zayas, the implicit yet crucial opposition between antithetical feminine archetypes, which correspond to the Eve-Mary opposition. Characteristically the negative Feminine is manifested in the figure of a sorceress, seductress, or wicked older woman; the positive Feminine, in a virginal figure who eventually consummates her holy marriage or enters a convent. The positive figures have a pure concept of love, seeing its end as marriage and procreation, while the negative archetypes, all facets of the "Terrible Mother," are libidinous and diabolical.

Zayas's rejection of corporeality can be interpreted as a kind of protest against a society in which woman was essentially a sexual being. The socially acceptable flight to the convent is a non-aggressive, less sensational version of other literary manifestations of rebellion, such as the bandolera.

363 Whitby, William M. "Calderón's El príncipe constante: Fénix's Role in the Ransom of Fernando's Body." BCom, 8 (Spring 1956), 1-4.

Fénix is identified with the city of Ceuta. Both are associated with the concept of beauty, and both are prizes which motivate the action. Fernando gives himself in ransom for Ceuta, and Ceuta in turn becomes Fernando's ransom price. This price is paid in full, symbolically, by the exchange of Fénix for Fernando's body.

364 _____. "Rosaura's Role in the Structure of La vida es sueño." HR, 28 (January 1960), 16-27. Also in Critical Essays, pp. 101-13.

Rosaura is, as E. M. Wilson (see entry 365) maintains, the key to Segismundo's conversion. Her presence awakens in the prince a consciousness of his true nature. The question of her identity is crucial to Segismundo's discovery of his own.

365 Wilson, E. M. "On La vida es sueño." Critical Essays, pp. 63-89.

Rosaura is the instrument of Segismundo's conversion; she completes what Clotaldo began. Like Clotaldo, Rosaura subordinates her life to principles. Both face their problems with constancy, unselfishness, and prudence and thus, do not ride to a fall like the other characters.

366 Wilson, Margaret. Tirso de Molina. Boston: Twayne, 1977.

Tirso's heroines possess an overpowering vitality. His best known formula is the heroine who pursues and angles for her man, assuming first a masculine and then a feminine identity. The young woman who falls in love with another of her sex, disguised as a man, is a stock device, but Tirso's interest in the theme is sufficient to make it a distinctive feature of his theater. El Aquiles raises the question of Lesbianism, to which there are very few references in the Golden Age theater. Tirso also shows some interest in figures who have an aversion to marriage, which can at times involve authentically individual characterization.

The real cause of María de Molina's triumph in La prudencia en la mujer is not prudence but supernatural power. The heroine has religious overtones and can be seen as an analogue of the Virgin Mary. With respect to Margarita of Quien no cae no se levanta, Wilson disagrees with those who object that Tirso exploits the protagonist's weakness as a means of luring her to heaven, giving the angel a physical attractiveness to which she cannot help but respond. The fact is that until Margarita's sexuality is itself won over and dedicated to God, her conversion cannot be complete.

367 Wiltrout, Ann E. "Las mujeres del Quijote." ACer, 12 (1973), 167-72.

In the first part of the Quixote, women are instruments in the creation of the dichotomies: reality/illusion, being/seeming, and truth/fiction.

368 _____. "Women in the Works of Antonio de Guevara." Neophil, 60 (October 1976), 525-33.

Since women always appear as a minor theme in Guevara's works, they are never accorded personal or philosophical depth. Guevara is far more interested in debating the feminist problem artistically than in contributing to its solution. Three basic stances with respect to women are discernible in Marco Aurelio y Reloj de príncipes and the Epístolas familiares. The most serious is that which provides rules for conjugal life and advice on the rearing and education of princesses. In Marco Aurelio, something of a misogynist's marriage manual, woman is not treated as a rational, adult human being but as a grown child who needs to be guided, protected, and disciplined. The second stance is basically erotic, dealing with Queen Faustina's less than favorable reputation, the emperor's interest in courtesans, and the advice which the latter offer other women. The last stance consists exclusively of ribald popular humor.

369 Yamuni, Vera. "La mujer en el pensamiento filosófico y literario." Anuario de Letras, México, 6 (1966-67), 179-200.

In the Renaissance, writers like Luis Vives and Fray Luis de León, who derive their ideas basically from St. Jerome, continue to enunciate ancient Christian ideals regarding women, even though more liberal and equitable principles have already been proclaimed, in particular by Castiglione. The difference between the two Spanish writers is relatively minimal and proportionate to the difference in their personal lives.

370 Zamora, Bonifacio. "¿Qué dice el Padre Gracián de la Reina Isabel?" Boletín de la Institución Fernán González, Burgos, Spain, 30 (1951), 725-39.

Gracián's Primores del héroe praises Isabel's modesty, virtue, and religion, and calls her the Catholic Amazon. El político recognizes her singular genuius and virile spirit. El criticón lauds her great judgment and recalls her way of life, which was never incompatible with domestic tasks. The Agudeza refers to her verbal wit, observing that she originated the expression tener buen gusto.

371 Zatlin Boring, Phyllis. "Women in the Quixote, Revisited." Studies in the Humanities, 4 (March 1974), 35-40.

Zatlin Boring contrasts Unamuno's views on the female characters in Don Quixote with those of Concha Espina. Espina, a feminist critic, finds in the novel women who are to be praised for their intelligence, goodness, loyalty, and bravery. Unamuno bypasses these characters and finds merit in prostitutes with a maternal heart, the willing woman-object Maritornes, and the least intelligent female character in the Quixote, doña Rodríguez.

Cervantes is not an antifeminist writer, as evidenced by the fact that he does not relegate women characters to the background to serve as decorative or useful objects; contend that women are the root of all evil; fill his pages with a handful of feminine stereotypes, while carefully individualizing male characters; or divide human qualities into masculine and feminine, with intelligence and bravery being masculine, elegance and weakness, feminine. A number of factors indicate that Cervantes was indeed a feminist. He portrays a liberated woman, Marcela, through whom he seems to proclaim a woman's right to freedom, the freedom to choose her own form of life. He indicates through characters such as Luscinda and Quiteria, that young women should have a voice in choosing a husband. He believes that women should be able to choose their own religion, provided they choose the right one. He sympathizes, as it were, with women's right to work. He sees marriage as partnerships. He portrays Luscinda and Dorotea as strong, admirable characters, while Fernando is deceitful and Cardenio, cowardly. He makes Dorotea's resourcefulness a high point of the work. Through Dulcinea, he debunks the stereotype of the lady from the courtly love tradition by showing that she does not exist.

372 Zimic, Stanislav. "Algunas observaciones sobre _La casa de los celos de Cervantes_." _Hispano_, no. 49 (September 1973), pp. 51-58.
The women of Cervantes's _comedia_, anticipating Alarcón's female characters in their opportunism, coldness, and calculation, convert men into the playthings of their whims. They also anticipate Dulcinea in the sense that their reality serves as ironic contrast to the exalted sentiments of their lovers.

Index of Authors and Anonymous Works

Included are anonymous works and those authors of primary works who are cited in the annotations. The numbers refer to the entries.

Acosta, Cristóbal de, 246, 281
Alcalá Yáñez, Jerónimo de, 143
Alemán, Mateo, 7, 49, 142, 143, 315
Arguijo, Juan de, 229
Avellaneda, Alonso F. de, 217, 224
Avellaneda, Lorenzo de, 301
Avila, Gaspar de, 275
Belmonte Bermúdez, Luis, 301
Bermúdez, Jerónimo, 12
Boscán, Juan, 272
Calderón de la Barca, Pedro, 16, 20, 21, 22, 32, 39, 41, 43, 44, 46, 53, 59, 69, 87, 91, 96, 97, 118, 120, 128, 137, 153, 155, 159, 160, 180, 216, 225, 234, 236, 237, 261, 298, 302, 310, 318, 321, 347, 353, 359, 363, 364, 365
Caro, Ana, 22, 235
Carvajal (Carabajal) y Saavedra, Mariana de, 42, 167
Castillejo, Cristóbal de, 157
Castillo Solórzano, Alonso de, 6, 22, 93, 143, 229, 287, 315
Castro, Guillén de, 1, 55, 188, 324, 361
Cervantes y Saavedra, Miguel de
Don Quixote, 8, 14, 16, 18, 19, 24, 26, 27, 28, 29, 34, 48, 57, 59, 61, 64, 65, 68, 75, 77, 78, 104, 105, 106, 110, 121, 123, 124, 133, 135, 144, 146, 147, 149, 157, 162, 163, 164, 165, 166, 177, 185, 198, 199, 201, 203, 204, 206, 207, 214, 217, 220, 224, 231, 240, 243, 245, 248, 249, 251, 255, 267, 268, 273, 278, 284, 285, 286, 295, 327, 329, 330, 336, 342, 343, 344, 367, 371
Novelas ejemplares, 8, 18, 19, 34, 50, 56, 70, 80, 81, 86, 92, 98, 116, 124, 139, 143, 177, 181, 196, 200, 247, 259, 264, 270, 271, 295, 299, 313, 326, 329
Other, 11, 18, 19, 25, 54, 63, 64, 74, 80, 87, 99, 103, 124, 125, 138, 168, 177, 183, 218, 240, 245, 246, 293, 295, 308, 320, 329, 347, 372
Céspedes y Meneses, Gonzalo, 126
Cueva, Juan de la, 237
Delicado, Francisco de, 30, 31, 82, 83, 95, 111, 148, 179, 292, 303, 304, 306, 357
Diamante, Juan Bautista, 13
Encina (Enzina), Juan del, 194, 209, 229, 338
Enríquez Gómez, Antonio, 143
Espinel, Vicente, 143, 258
Espinosa, Juan de, 281
Espinosa, Pedro de, 258
Estrella de Sevilla, La, 47, 313, 322

Gallego, Manuel de, 229
García, Carlos, 143
Garcilaso de la Vega, 15, 337, 352
Godínez, Felipe, 112
Góngora, Luis de Argote y, 228, 246, 311, 356
Gracián, Baltasar, 137, 171, 246, 297, 313, 370
Granados y Mosquera, Diego, 301
Guevara, Antonio de, 100, 113, 345, 346, 368
Herrero, Pedro, 301
Huarte de San Juan, Juan, 113, 246
Lazarillo de Tormes, La vida de, 7, 49, 306, 315, 360
León, Luis de, 41, 88, 100, 101, 113, 246, 289, 293, 297, 306, 313, 330, 347, 369
Lobo Lasso de la Vega, Gabriel, 12, 188, 275
López de Ubeda, Francisco, 6, 7, 35, 36, 143, 223, 304, 339
Luján, Pedro, 281
Luna, Juan de, 143, 179
Martí, Juan, 143
Martínez de Meneses, Antonio, 301
Mexía de la Cerda, Luis (Juan?), 12
Mira de Amescua, Antonio, 45, 219, 234, 250, 252, 324
Montemayor, Jorge de, 25, 44, 67, 205, 260, 276, 354
Monteser, Francisco Antonio de, 301
Moreto, Agustín, 37, 52, 172, 183, 234, 235, 237, 301, 338
Pérez de Montalbán (Montalván), Juan, 253, 258, 313, 324
Pinto Delgado, João (Juan), 112
Polo, Gaspar Gil, 226, 276, 314
Quevedo, Francisco de, 7, 16, 41, 49, 50, 87, 102, 134, 143, 202, 208, 229, 246, 259, 297, 308, 313
Quiñones de Benavente, Luis, 16, 296
Rebolledo, Bernardino de, 69
Rojas Zorrilla, Francisco de, 56, 131, 183, 228, 229, 230, 302, 325
Rueda, Lope de, 44, 288
Ruiz de Alarcón y Mendoza, Juan, 20, 21, 87, 117, 216, 237, 269, 347, 372
Saavedra Guzmán, Antonio de, 275
Salas Barbadillo, Alonso Jerónimo de, 6, 66, 143, 176, 223, 304, 315
Salazar y Torres, Agustín de, 244
Sedeño, Juan de, 312
Silva, Feliciano de, 292
Solís, Antonio de, 137, 301
Suárez de Alarcón, Juan, 12
Teresa de Jesús, Santa, 88, 246, 254, 290, 345
Timoneda, Juan de, 280
Tirso de Molina (Gabriel Téllez), 17, 20, 21, 22, 40, 44, 45, 59, 70, 85, 87, 89, 108, 109, 117, 122, 125, 126, 130, 132, 140, 145, 173, 195, 197, 210, 211, 212, 216, 221, 234, 237, 239, 252, 256, 261, 265, 266, 277, 308, 316, 324, 335, 347, 351, 353, 366
Torquemada, Antonio de, 188
Turia, Ricardo de, 235
Vega y Carpio, Lope de
  Dramatic works, 10, 13, 20, 21, 22, 38, 44, 45, 58, 60, 79, 84, 86, 87, 94, 107, 109, 112, 117, 118, 119, 125, 129, 141, 146, 152, 154, 158, 161, 170, 172, 175, 182, 191, 192, 216, 227, 228, 229, 234, 235, 237, 238, 241, 252, 256, 261, 263, 274, 277, 288, 291, 296, 297, 302, 305, 309, 324, 328, 334, 335, 338, 347, 348, 349, 355
  Other, 2, 4, 10, 62, 120, 136, 184, 188, 213, 215, 222, 232, 258, 262, 274, 294, 300, 308, 319, 331, 332, 348, 349
Vélez de Guevara, Luis, 12, 13, 23, 45, 50, 72, 76, 234, 252, 282, 283, 324
Vicente, Gil, 190
Villalón, Cristóbal de, 306, 345, 346

Virués, Cristóbal de, 97, 188, 237
Zabaleta, Juan de, 293
Zárate, Francisco de, 297
Zayas y Sotomayor, María de, 9, 33, 70, 71, 114, 115, 171, 178, 186, 233, 242, 279, 280, 281, 317, 323, 340, 341, 362

Index of Topics

The numbers refer to the annotated entries.

Themes

Beauty, 2, 25, 56, 67, 74, 75, 113, 136, 187, 218, 228, 270, 308, 313
Education or culture, 10, 41, 233, 246, 281, 297, 345, 347
False accusation, 280, 329, 333, 334, 335 (See also Zayas y Sotomayor)
Fashions or customs, 41, 42, 87, 242, 293
Feminism, 9, 10, 22, 41, 70, 92, 103, 125, 148, 171, 178, 186, 188, 189, 209, 230, 233, 234, 235, 236, 237, 246, 276, 281, 290, 297, 317, 325, 351, 354, 359, 360, 368, 371
Freedom in love, 20, 25, 41, 42, 64, 77, 144, 145, 159, 163, 191, 207, 230, 246, 281, 325, 329, 336, 371
Honor, 35, 41, 46, 53, 87, 89, 92, 125, 159, 160, 180, 191, 210, 225, 230, 234, 239, 246, 247, 261, 271, 280, 285, 302, 323, 329, 336, 341, 347, 355, 358
Intellectual capacity, 9, 15, 19, 101, 103, 113, 114, 161, 171, 188, 230, 237, 246, 290, 323, 348
Lesbianism, 23, 237, 366
Misogyny, 8, 10, 70, 87, 102, 125, 134, 142, 143, 179, 202, 206, 208, 276, 297, 306, 315, 339, 348, 360, 368
Natural inferiority or weakness, 10, 88, 94, 101, 113, 142, 156, 290, 306, 330, 368
Nudity, 183, 228, 230
Woman's role, 7, 22, 41, 46, 49, 52, 92, 94, 100, 101, 113, 137, 144, 145, 158, 161, 167, 171, 178, 191, 197, 204, 209, 235, 237, 241, 246, 270, 281, 290, 297, 307, 321, 338, 345, 347, 351, 362, 368, 369, 370, 371

Types

Adulteress, 127, 172, 193, 202, 229, 241, 329
Amazon, 137, 212, 237, 370
Bandolera, 45, 85, 234, 237, 252, 282, 362
Biblical figures, 112, 128, 129, 130, 132, 140, 190, 277, 305, 316, 319
Boba, 119, 146, 158, 161
Burlada, 108, 126, 188, 210, 239, 252, 341, 353
Buscona, 202, 285, 315
Celestina type or procuress, 30, 31, 41, 66, 77, 83, 90, 141, 150, 156, 176, 179, 194, 215, 232, 238, 244, 250, 257, 262, 285, 292, 328, 329, 331
Courtesan, 30, 31, 41, 82, 368
Criada, 41, 126, 169, 238, 269, 329, 332
Culta, 4, 20, 37, 52, 87, 119, 158, 161, 208, 258, 297, 348, 349

Dama, 78, 89, 126, 157, 169, 187, 215, 249, 288, 338, 339
Dueña, 8, 16, 41, 90, 176, 202, 208, 238
Enamorada, 10, 19, 41, 44, 65, 84, 89, 145, 169, 174, 175, 205, 226, 230, 263, 269, 285, 288, 325, 326, 329, 341
Esquiva, 37, 44, 52, 115, 144, 149, 163, 209, 226, 235, 237, 329, 338, 366
Fregona, 8, 34, 56, 98, 196, 208, 291
Gypsy, 41, 80, 124, 264, 271
Historical or legendary figures: non-Spanish, 69, 96, 97, 127, 151, 188, 189, 203, 229, 245, 261, 275, 294, 359
Historical or legendary figures: Spanish, 1, 12, 55, 72, 76, 89, 140, 173, 174, 184, 221, 253, 256, 275, 277, 284, 301, 361, 370 (See also Saint)
Hypocrite, 90, 127, 150, 154, 195, 202, 208, 262, 277, 285, 306
Jewess or conversa, 138, 184, 232, 304
Maga, 25, 120, 260, 314
Melindrosa, 152, 256, 296
Mooress, 3, 121, 124, 193, 243, 245, 284, 329
Mother, 12, 20, 39, 41, 42, 49, 56, 92, 99, 113, 149, 152, 153, 154, 155, 172, 173, 176, 215, 238, 263, 277, 299, 306, 324, 356, 358
Mujer varonil or virago, 23, 37, 44, 79, 88, 97, 137, 193, 204, 234, 235, 237, 250, 253, 269, 290, 301, 302, 329, 341, 370 (See also Amazon, Bandolera, Esquiva, Serrana, Warrior)
Mujer vestida de hombre, La, 9, 20, 21, 23, 44, 59, 73, 89, 140, 146, 172, 206, 211, 250, 288, 351, 366
Mythological figures, 37, 39, 52, 54, 62, 91, 120, 137, 149, 153, 155, 192, 213, 230, 231, 241, 329, 337 (See also Amazon)
Nun, 41, 88, 202, 208, 211, 253, 254, 265, 290
Old woman, 41, 194, 202, 208, 270
Pícara, 6, 7, 30, 31, 35, 36, 41, 83, 143, 223, 287, 304, 339
Précieuse, 41, 87, 297
Prostitute, 31, 34, 83, 92, 148, 156, 200, 202, 285, 304, 306, 315, 371
Queen, 52, 69, 96, 97, 99, 128, 131, 140, 173, 188, 221, 277, 350, 359, 368, 370
Saint, 13, 102, 131, 186, 211
Seductress, 51, 116, 142, 143, 227, 241, 273, 344, 362
Serrana, 45, 51, 126, 157, 234, 251, 252, 282, 283 (See also Bandolera)
Shepherdess, 14, 15, 25, 26, 54, 57, 64, 65, 124, 126, 144, 149, 164, 168, 203, 207, 226, 231, 240, 260, 276, 300, 329
Sinner converted, 45, 69, 85, 95, 184, 252, 301, 366
Victim, 9, 12, 22, 33, 53, 70, 71, 76, 86, 92, 98, 107, 115, 125, 126, 141, 142, 159, 160, 171, 178, 184, 186, 188, 189, 199, 225, 229, 234, 236, 241, 243, 257, 261, 283, 301, 304, 307, 321, 323, 324, 340, 344, 353, 360 (See also Burlada, False accusation, Honor)
Warrior or soldier, 44, 69, 237, 250, 253, 319 (See also Amazon)
Widow, 42, 113, 118, 152, 154, 167, 188, 236, 277, 319, 347
Wife, 41, 53, 70, 101, 113, 131, 132, 161, 173, 193, 289, 306, 340, 355, 368
Witch or sorceress, 50, 99, 120, 149, 177, 208, 227, 241, 259, 267, 329, 362 (See also Celestina type)
Woman as muse, 272, 331
Woman as symbol
Dulcinea, 24, 28, 57, 61, 65, 68, 78, 81, 104, 106, 110, 123, 124, 133, 135, 147, 149, 162, 164, 185, 199,

217, 220, 224, 248, 251, 255, 268, 273, 278, 286, 327, 342
Preciosa, 56, 81, 116, 139, 168
Rosaura, 32, 43, 180, 298
Others, 43, 47, 48, 56, 57, 58, 91, 95, 98, 99, 108, 111, 112, 129, 132, 162, 168, 199, 273, 320, 357, 363, 366
Writer, 4, 171, 258, 348